THE COUNTRY HOUSEWIFE

THE COUNTRY HOUSEWIFE

A Compendium and Anthology
of Country Lore

Simone Sekers

HODDER AND STOUGHTON
LONDON SYDNEY AUCKLAND TORONTO

Illustrations by
Rodney Shackell.

British Library Cataloguing in Publication Data

Sekers, Simone
    The country housewife.

    1. Country life—Great Britain—History
    2. Great Britain—Social life and customs—
        19th century   3. Great Britain—Social life
        and customs—18th century
    I. Title
    941'.00973'4   DA533

    ISBN 0 340 28336 X

Hodder and Stoughton Editorial Office: 47 Bedford Square,
London WC1B 3DP.

✌ *Contents* ✌

❧ *Acknowledgments* ❧

I am very grateful to all those who helped me compile this book, and in particular—my mother Diana Caplat, who taught me a good deal about the subject from an early age; my husband David, indefatigable in his search for old books on the subject, and his support and patience; my daughter Lucy, for her help as a housewife while I was hard at work; Vera Beck of Cockermouth, who has helped my housewifery for many years; David and Angela Winkworth and Terry Lee, also of Cockermouth, who helped me with the technicalities; Nerine Abbott, Betty Allen and Jean Antrobus of Quarry Bank Mill, Styal, who gave me invaluable hints, advice and good examples; Vera Holt and Sheila Hallas for their help with this book, and Francis Connell who gave me the time to write it; the Editor of *The Countryman* for his permission to reproduce the map on page 69; and finally, Richard Bradley who, in 1732, published a book called *The Country Housewife*, which was the inspiration behind this book.

❧ *Introduction* ❧

As I was compiling this book, I had two mental pictures: one was of the Old Country Housewife—ample, aproned, with a basket of eggs on her arm and a flock of glossy hens around her feet; her backdrop a substantial farm house, the open door revealing a kitchen with a polished range, a white scrubbed table on which a freshly baked pie of immense proportions was cooling, beside it a primly frilled yellow-crumbed ham and a quart jug of cider. The other was of the New Country Housewife—slimmer than her predecessor, in jeans and anorak, checking that she has her card for the cash-and-carry as she walks towards the car; her backdrop is the same farm house, but the hens are housed in a battery shed, and the open kitchen door reveals a Rayburn in place of the range, and a Formica-topped table crowded with, among other things, a packet of cornflakes, a jar of instant coffee, and a half-empty tub of polyunsaturate margarine.

Both pictures contain more than a grain of truth (after all, I know the New Country Housewife very well indeed); however much I tried to find drawbacks to the Old Country Life—and I found many, particularly when I read of poverty and starvation in the Victorian countryside, disease and death in the 'picturesque' thatched cottages now so sought after by weekenders—its tranquil self-sufficiency and the peace of a life geared to the slow moving wheel of the seasons remained irresistibly more attractive than our New Country Life. Now the wheel of the seasons spins faster and the seasons themselves have become blurred; with freezers and intensive farming methods it is possible to eat eggs and fresh meat all the year round—the inherited skills of generations of frugal housewives are no longer of vital necessity.

The Old Country Housewife was tied hand and foot, either by responsibility or poverty, to feeding, clothing and doctoring herself and her household. In the sixteenth, seventeenth and even in the eighteenth centuries, flax had to be grown in order to provide linen sheets and smocks, or there were no sheets and smocks to be had; first wool had to be shorn from the sheep to provide woollen clothing or the family went cold. In the nineteenth century, these things could be bought—there were others who manufactured the linen and woollen cloth, but money to pay for them was harder to come by, as mechanisation on farms created at best low wages, at worst, unemployment and no wages at all. Food continued to be home-produced until the cottager was no longer allowed his pig; the demise of this important member of the family heralded the rise of cheap but unhealthy food: meat pastes, factory bread, and the like, which invaded the country villages by means of the carriers' carts from the towns. Vegetables were still grown on the allotments, but by the First World War tinned food was to be seen on the shelves of the village shops. The Women's Institutes did much to encourage the continuation of the Old Country

Housewife's way of life, and their advice was of enormous help, particularly during the last war, when so many of the old skills were kept alive by the network of WI branches throughout the country.

The New Country Housewife is as tied as her predecessor, but by different calls upon her responsibilities. Her contribution to the economy is often outside the house, rather than within; a very large number of villages are empty during the day as both the New Country Housewife and her husband commute to work in the town. Their children will be at school in their own village if they are lucky, but more often than not they will have to be taken to another larger school which has absorbed children from a wide radius. Much of the life of the twentieth-century country dweller's time is spent in the car, as bus services dwindle and die and village shops close. A vicious circle results for, as more cars are needed to ferry children to school and the parents to work, fewer services are thought to be necessary.

The responsibilities of the conscientious New Country Housewife towards her village have not changed all that much. The Old Country Housewife, if she were the Squire's wife, might have taught catechism and sewing to the village girls, would almost certainly have cared for the sick, old and poor, and meddled—well-meaningly—in the lives of her husband's tenants. If she were the Parson's wife, her duties would have been much the same, only carried out in the shadow of the squire's lady, and often on an income almost as low as that of the poorest parishioner she helped. As the Farmer's wife, she would have been responsible for the families of the farm's labourers, as well as for the 'lighter' farming tasks—cheese and butter making, poultry and bee-keeping. As for the Labourer's wife, her world was circumscribed by the struggle to feed and clothe her family and herself. Now the New Country Housewife, as the Squire's wife, will sit on the parish council, become a JP, help with Meals-on-Wheels, and all the many fund-raising activities still necessary despite the welfare state; she is likely to be a hospital visitor, maybe a prison visitor, too. She is probably a member of the National Trust, helping to arrange flowers and repair embroideries in the nearest stately home. As the Vicar's wife her duties are more onerous and her income much smaller. At least the vicarage is now a more manageable size—often a neat bungalow built in the garden of the rambling old vicarage, which leaves her more time for running playgroups, helping her husband run the youth club, and being a sort of unofficial marriage guidance counsellor, citizen's advice bureau and amateur psychiatrist rolled into one. As for the Farmer's wife, her duties have been halved; total mechanisation has reduced the farm work force to an eighth of what it was even forty years ago; specialisation in farming means that a farm will keep sheep, or a dairy or beef herd, or grow cereals, but not all together. There are many farmers' wives who raise their own flock of hens, to sell free-range eggs at the farm gate, or who breed horses, or dogs, or rare sheep, but these are hobbies, and not an essential contribution to the farm's economy. And as the Labourer's wife, her life is immeasurably easier. A farm worker now earns a respectable wage; he can run a car, and his wife probably works as a nurse in the local hospital, or teaches in the village school, so their joint income enables them to lead a life of luxury undreamed of by the Victorian farm labourer.

But it was to the old way of life that I was drawn, by talk of 'the good old' 'bad old' days from people old enough to remember, and by the reading of countless old cookery books, herbals, and manuals. One of the most nostalgic of my sources was Henry Stephens' *Book of the Farm*—a two-volume compendium of every aspect of farming in the British Isles in the mid-nineteenth century, from weather lore to how a farmer should spend his spare time, from the wild flowers found on various soils to the most cost-effective way of feeding cattle in winter. My other favourite source is Richard Bradley's *The Country Housewife*, after which this book is named. I was fortunate to find a copy of the 1753 edition in a bookshop in Marlborough ten years ago and it has been a constant source of interest, pleasure and amusement. The recipes, for the most part, need little adaptation, although the medicines are often alarming, calling as they do for spirits of vitriol or quantities of snails. Bradley intended his book to be the 'Lady's Director, for every month of the Year, both in the Frugal Management of the House and the Delights and Profits of the Farm', and from his book and many others I have taken snippets of fact and custom to try to build up a composite picture of the lives of Old Country Housewives for the interest of the New.

This is not a 'how to be' book, but a 'how it was' ragbag of bits and pieces which I hope will prove to be rather like an armchair rummage through an attic or barn on a wet afternoon, when domestic relics of the past turn up and prove, when the dust, and cobwebs have been brushed away, to be as useful and absorbing as they were to our ancestors.

Simone Sekers
Cockermouth, and Styal, 1982

❧ *Conversion Tables* ❧

Weights			Measurements	
¹/₂ oz	10 g (grams)		¹/₈ in	3 mm (millimetre)
1	25		¹/₄	¹/₂ cm (centimetre)
1¹/₂	40		¹/₂	1
2	50		³/₄	2
2¹/₂	60		1	2.5
3	75		1¹/₄	3
4	110		1¹/₂	4
4¹/₂	125		1³/₄	4.5
5	150		2	5
6	175		3	7.5
7	200		4	10
8	225		5	13
9	250		6	15
10	275		7	18
12	350		8	20
1 lb	450		9	23
1¹/₂	700		10	25.5
2	900		11	28
3	1 kg 350 g		12	30

Volume

2 fl oz	55 ml	1³/₄ pints	1 litre
3 fl oz	75	4 gills (1 pint)	570 ml
5 fl oz (¹/₄ pint)	150	2 pints (1 quart)	1.140 litre
¹/₂ pint	275	4 quarts (1 gallon)	4.560
³/₄ pint	425	2 gallons (1 peck)	9.120
1 pint	570	4 pecks (1 bushel)	36.480

All these are *approximate* conversions, which have been either rounded up or down.

Temperature

Electricity and Solid Fuel	Gas Mark	Degrees Fahrenheit	Degrees Centigrade
Cool	$1/4$	200	100
Cool	$1/4$	225	110
Cool	$1/4 - 1/2$	250	120
Very Slow	1	275	140
Slow	2	300	150
Slow	3	325	160
Moderate	4	350	180
Moderate	5	375	190
Moderately hot	6	400	200
Hot	7	425	220
Very hot	8	450	230
Very hot	9	475	250

These conversion tables have been worked out as practical cooking approximations.

🌿 *The Country Garden* 🌿

In March and in April from morning till night
In sowing and seeding good housewives delight
To have her a garden or other like spot
To trim up the house and to furnish the pot
                                        Thomas Tusser, 1573

A flower garden was once a luxury, only to be afforded if
there was enough ground left over from growing the staples
such as potatoes, cabbages and onions. Most farm labourers
would expect to be provided with an allotment which went
with their tied cottage, but even so there was little space for
roses or pinks. The resourceful housewife grew flowers up
the walls of the cottage, and on the windowsills—honeysuckle, jasmine, climbing roses, geraniums and mignonette
in pots, wallflowers and hollyhocks close against the wall.

The only other plants apart from vegetables which were allowed space were herbs, often threefold in their usefulness: 'to furnish the pot', to use medicinally, and lastly to 'trim up the house'. Marigolds are a typical example—their petals coloured cheese and were added to soups and broths to 'revive the spirits', the leaves soothed insect bites, and the flowers added colour to both house and garden.

The more extensive the garden, the greater the space allowed for herbs, either in formal herb gardens, neatly laid out with gravel paths and box hedges, or in more informal enclosures where they grew unchecked to supply the still-room with ingredients for medicines, toilet waters and pot pourri.

The vegetable garden was, as it is now, a male preserve—the vegetables grown for size either to satisfy the family's hunger, or to compete with fellow gardeners; the competitive element would seem timeless. Old fashioned gardeners still prefer their onions strong enough to 'blow the door shut with a breath', and radishes 'with a bit of fire to them', like the Woods' Early Frame radish which I tried this year, a variety now omitted from catalogues. The battle is on to preserve these old varieties, and organisations such as the Henry Doubleday Research Association are pioneers in safe-guarding 'antique' vegetables from the obliterating blanket of Common Market regulations. Gardens growing such vegetables can be seen at Wells (Somerset), Wimborne (Dorset), and Styal (Cheshire).

The Henry Doubleday Research Association advocates keeping your own seed, which older generations of gardeners did as a matter of course. If you are willing to forego the 'advantages' of hybridisation, the results are extremely worthwhile; I have just been admiring some vigorous broad beans, grown by a neighbour from four-year-old seed, kept in a paper bag at the back of a cupboard and forgotten until this year's spring cleaning.

16

Fruit growing was often left to those with suitably large gardens and gardeners to help with the forcing of peaches and nectarines, the pruning and training of espaliers, cordons and fans (some fascinating examples in the art of fruit-tree-training can be seen in the gardens at Erddig, the National Trust property near Wrexham); farm gardens produced the more utilitarian fruits such as raspberries and gooseberries, apples, pears and plums, and even a small cottage garden might contain an old apple tree, or a pear tree grown against the end wall. My own favourite gardens are those where flowers, fruit, vegetables and herbs grow together, often sharing the same beds where space is limited, and where mown grass paths between the rows of currant bushes, leeks and lettuces provide a calm atmosphere in a busy and productive place; gardens like the one Thomas Tusser suggests, where:

> The gooseberry, respis, and roses all three,
> With strawberries beneath them, do trimly agree.

🌿 *The Herb Garden* 🌿

Growing

Most herbs prefer a soil that is not too acid, so before planning a herb garden, buy or borrow a soil-testing kit. If the PH level is 6.0, or thereabouts, the acidity will need to be corrected by the addition of ground limestone at the rate of 8 oz per square yard (if the PH level is above 7.0, add a little peat to counteract the alkalinity).

April—Sowing Pot-herbs. Thyme, sweet-marjoram, savory and hyssop should now be sown.—Parsley, chervil, and coriander may yet be sown—Sow borage and bugloss where wanted; also clary, angelica, lovage, scurvy-grass, caraway, and carduus; burnet, sorrel and marigolds, fennel and dill. Plant rooted slips of balm, penny-royal, and chamomile &c in the herbary—Root slips of tansey, and tarragon may yet be planted; likewise pot-marjoram, burnet, chives and sorrel. Plant top slips of sage, they will grow freely. This is also a good season to propagate by slips, lavender, for its flowers to distil, & also rue, rosemary and lavender cotton, in smaller portions for domestic occasions; also plant wormwood.

Thomas Mawe and John Abercrombie, 1829

Grow lemon thyme as well as the ordinary variety, to use with chicken and fish dishes.

Grow tarragon, basil, chervil and fennel for more subtle flavours. Make sure that you grow the true French tarragon—it is tender and needs protection in the winter even in the south, but the flavour is incomparably better than that of the hardier Russian tarragon. If you are proud of your flourishing tarragon plant, which even managed to survive the winter of 1981–2, then you have Russian tarragon. Basil is an annual which should be grown in pots, in a greenhouse, or on a sunny windowsill. Chervil flourishes cheerfully and will seed itself, often giving a supply through the whole of a mild winter. Bronze fennel is an attractive addition to a border and seems to have as good a flavour as the green.

Grow chives, to add a mild onion flavour to cooked dishes, salads and soups. The flowers are pretty, too, and make a good edging plant for the vegetable garden.

18

Grow parsley, another good edging plant. Boiling water poured on to the seeds as you sow them helps speed up germination.

Try potting your surplus herbs and offering them to your local health-food shop to sell—they are often only too glad to have fresh herbs.

Usage and Superstition

A pot of scented geraniums on the windowsill stops flies from coming through an open window (see page 29 for more details on varieties).

Myrtis communis, or myrtle, was traditionally included in wedding bouquets because it was the sacred herb of Aphrodite, according to Greek mythology. It is an aromatic shrub with fragrant white flowers in late summer which needs a warm and sheltered spot. The dried leaves are an important ingredient of pot pourri.

In Cambridgeshire, the periwinkle was planted in the garden of the house of newly weds for luck. Culpeper says, 'Venus owns this herb—the leaves, eaten by man and wife together causes love between them.' And that, 'the young tops made into a conserve are serviceable in that troublesome complaint, the nightmare.'

Lily of the valley are said to thrive in the vicinity of Solomon's seal, 'their husbands'; certainly both plants like the same shady position. The roots of Solomon's seal are 'commended extremely for an outward application against bruises', and the flowers of lily of the valley, made into a tea and taken regularly, 'is excellent against all nervous complaints'.

Robinson's New Family Herbal, c1870

Woodrooffe hathe leaves set round like a star, or the rowell of a spurre: the floures grow at the top of the stems, of a white colour, and of a very sweet smell, as is the rest of the herbs, which being made up into garlands or bundles, and hanging up in houses in the heat of Summer, doth very well attemper the aire, coole and make fresh the place, to the delight and comfort of such as are therein.

John Gerard, 1633

It makes delightful ground cover too, in dappled shade.

Rue is said to grow best if stolen.

'Plant fennel, plant troubles,' goes the old saying, which can be interpreted to mean that fennel has a limiting effect on the growth of any plants near it, although I have not found this to be so. It is far truer of sweet cicely, which is best admired from a distance and not brought into the garden, where it will colonise rapidly and vigorously.

Take your bay tree with you when you move house or you will 'leave luck behind'. It is best planted in a tub in any case, as in many areas it needs winter protection.

A bunch of washed mint dipped quickly in and out of a jug of milk is thought to stop the milk curdling in thundery weather.

Hang a bunch of mint in the larder to keep flies away; have a jug of mint and marigolds on your kitchen table—the marigolds will absorb cooking smells.

Mint leaves will keep flies off raw meat—change the leaves frequently. It is remarkable how many butchers still have a large jug of mint in their shops in the summer, despite modern methods of fly prevention.

It is meet that our Housewife know that from the eight of the Kalends of the month of April, unto the eight of the Kalends of July, all manner of herbs and leaves are in that time most in strength and of the greatest vertue to be used, and put in all manner of Medicines, also from the eight of the Kalends of July, unto the eight of the Kalends of October, the Stalkes, stems and hard branches of every herb and plant is most in strength to be used in Medicines; and from the eight of the Kalends of October, unto the eight of the Kalends of April, all manner of roots of herbs and plants are most of strength and virtue to be used in all manner of Medicines.

Gervase Markham, 1653

Pick your herbs for drying on a dry day before the sun is at its height but after the dew has dried. Make them up into small bunches and hang them up in a dry airy place, or layer them between sheets of newspaper to dry in an airing cupboard. When they are absolutely dry, strip the leaves from the stalks and store them either in brown glass jars (to exclude the light as well as the air), or in cotton bags with drawstring tops. This last method is particularly useful for the culinary herbs, as the bags, each with the name of the herb it contains written on in marking ink, can be hung on a hook near the cooker, and can be washed and re-used many times.

Recipes

Frying Herbs, as dressed in Staffordshire
Clean and drain a good quantity of spinach leaves, two large handfuls of parsley, and a handful of green onions. Chop the parsley and onions, and sprinkle them among the spinach. Set them all on to stew with some salt and a bit of butter the size of a walnut: shake the pan when it begins to grow warm, and let it be closely covered over a slow fire till done enough. It is served with slices of broiled calves' liver, small rashers of bacon, and eggs fried; the latter on the herbs, the others in a separate dish.

Mrs Rundell, 1818

Cumberland Herb Pudding
Chop a handful each of young nettle tops, dandelion leaves, Easter ledges (bistort), watercress, currant leaves, sorrel. Mix with a handful of barley, add a beaten egg or two to mix, season well and tie in a floured cloth (or put in a greased basin) and steam for 2½–3 hours. Serve very hot with a knob of butter.

A lighter version, quite delicious with a roast capon for Easter Sunday lunch, is to prepare the herbs by steaming them until tender, then chopping them finely with a hard-boiled egg or two, adding seasoning and enough raw beaten

22

egg to bind the mixture lightly together, and steaming this in a buttered basin for ¾ of an hour. Turn out to serve. Ground-elder is sometimes added to this, but it does have a powerful flavour which cancels out the more delicate herbs.

Another traditional Easter dish is a tansy, called after the herb which flavours it. The camphor-like flavour is not to everyone's taste, but it used to be very popular, perhaps because 'the flowers, dried, powdered, and mixed with treacle, are a common medicine for worms, and they visibly destroy them'.

To make a Tansy

Take eight Whites and twenty Yolks of Eggs, beat them well and strain them into a Quart of thick Cream and six Naples Biskets grated: colour it to your Mind with Juice of Spinage, and a very little Tansey; sweeten it with fine Sugar to your Palate, then add Nutmeg; you must butter the Dish, and then likewise butter a Sheet of Paper, lay it over your Dish, and pour into it the Tansey; set it in an Oven fit for baking Custards, and when it is done, turn it out upon a Pye-plate, dredge it over with Sugar, and garnish the Dish with Slices of Orange and Lemon.

Richard Bradley, 1753

For a twentieth-century tansy, use half a pint of single cream, 2 large eggs, 2 oz sponge cake crumbs, ½ tablespoon of finely chopped tansy leaves, 1 oz sugar and a grating of nutmeg. Follow the old recipe, buttering the dish well, but omitting the paper, and bake in a roasting-tin half full of water at 350°F for 45 minutes. Serve cold. I do not colour mine, preferring a natural creamy yellow colour to a sallow green.

23

Mint Sauce

Chop the leaves finely and mix with a tablespoon or two of honey, then leave for an hour. Add lemon juice to moisten, just before serving.

Italian Mint Sauce

Put a large handful each of parsley and mint into a blender, together with 2 large cloves of garlic, a dozen tablespoonfuls of olive oil, the juice of half a lemon, salt and pepper and 2 tablespoonfuls of grated Parmesan. Blend until fine, and serve with cold pasta, or fish, or a simple tomato salad. The combination of the two herbs and the Parmesan produces a flavour not unlike that of basil—very useful for those who find basil difficult to grow.

Grand Sallet

All sorts of Good herbs, the little leaves of red sage, the smallest leaves of Sorrel and the leaves of Parsley picked very small, tear some white cabbage leaves, the youngest and smallest leaves of spinage, some leaves of burnet, the smallest leaves of lettice, white endive and chervil all finely picked, washed and swung in a strainer, or clean napkin and well drained from the water, then dish it in a clean scoured dish and about the centre capers, currants, olives, lemons cerved and sliced, boiled beetroots, carved and slic'd and dished round also, with good oil and Vinegar.

Robert May, 1671

Other salad recipes of the seventeenth and eighteenth centuries recommended 'cowslip buds, violet-flowers and leaves, strawberry leaves'. Although I would not suggest cowslip buds now they have become so rare, the first young leaf buds of the hawthorn, called 'bread and cheese' by country children, are a delicious salad ingredient, coming at a time when fresh greenery is scarce, with a sweet, nutty flavour and crisp texture.

Dandelion and bacon salad is an old country dish, but the dandelions need blanching in the spring. Either tie the leaves together with raffia (at weekly intervals, to ensure a continuity of supply), or put pieces of slate or tile over the plants. Pick, wash and dry the leaves; cut some unsmoked bacon into cubes and fry until crisp, then add them to the leaves; pour a spoonful or two of vinegar into the fat remaining in the pan, let it sizzle, then add it to the salad and mix well.

❧ *The Flower Garden* ❧

March—Sowing hardy annual Flowers—Sow in borders and other compartments, pots &c the seeds of hardy annuals, such as large and dwarf annual sunflower, oriental mallow, lavatera, persicaria, Venice mallow, larkspur, flos Adonis, sweet sultan, large rose and blue and yellow lupines, convolvulus major and minor, sweet-scented peas, Tangier peas, nasturtiums, the Spanish nigella, purple and white candytuft, virgin stock, Venus's looking glass, Venus navelwort, double poppy, Lobel's catchfly, dwarf lychnis, snails, caterpillars, ten-week stocks, and mignonette, and various others.

Thomas Mawe and John Abercrombie, 1829

Some of the flowers in this list are familiar, others are now listed as 'wild', such as Venus looking glass (*Legousia hybrida*); snails and caterpillars could be called hardy annuals, although I think snails are perennials. It is as if Mr Abercrombie compiled this list while gazing into his own borders, simply writing down all he saw; rather reassuring for the amateur gardener.

I have grown the 'old fashioned' sweet peas for the first time this summer and, while the flowers are smaller, the scent is much stronger than that offered by modern varieties. Many of the seed catalogues list these old kinds, and although germination is slow, it is worth persevering.

Honeysuckles of the several Species will succeed well from Cuttings, planted in a Bed, tolerably expos'd, at this Time (August). Let the . . . Honeysuckles . . . be planted 4″ deep. The common Practice of laying Honeysuckles is more troublesome, and the Cuttings, with tolerable Management, succeed as well.

John Hill, 1757

Edging Plants

The old gardening books recommend box most strongly, but it needs clipping frequently for neatness. Thrift, daisies, London Pride, pinks and strawberries were also advocated. Of the strawberries, the alpine variety, Baron Solemacher, is one of the neatest as it produces no runners; the flavour of the fruit is an added bonus. Flax (*linum usitatissimum*) makes a beautiful blue edging, in flower all summer and easily kept neat by clipping. It is particularly good for edging beds of old roses, as the blue is very sympathetic to the soft and subtle colours.

Roses

The old roses have a short season, but compensate by their glorious scent and decorative foliage; some also have a second flowering, while others produce spectacular hips in early autumn. Their petals, dried, form the most important part of pot pourri; for good stockists of the old varieties, see the list at the end of this chapter. Here is a short list from the many available—* denotes a variety that withstands rain, an important consideration in some parts of the country.

Fantin Latour: full, pale pink.

Blanchefleur: pinkish white and sweetly scented.

Blanc Double de Coubert: single pure white and strongly scented, a rugosa with good hips.

Old Pink Moss*: the old moss rose of cottage gardens, with a wonderful scent.

Ispahan: a damask rose with a longer season than some, and light green leaves which contrast well with the bright pink flowers.

Souvenir du Docteur Jamain and Château de Close Vougeot*: both dark wine-red and powerfully scented. Docteur Jamain fades in bright sunshine.

Gipsy Boy*: very dark purplish-crimson.

NL 849*: a rich crimson-pink damask rose, repeat flowering.

Rosa Mundi: striped and blotched in pink, white and crimson; one of the oldest of the old roses, said to be twelfth century.

Sweet briars: here the foliage is scented—a sweet briar hedge is impenetrably thorny, but is inclined to be leggy; try training a honeysuckle or clematis round its ankles. Meg Merrilees has single crimson flowers, Lady Penzance has single, buff-yellow flowers.

Gloire de Dijon and Albertine: two lovely ramblers, sweetly scented, the first pale apricot and the last coppery pink. Albertine is not good in wet weather, as the petals turn brown and soggy and cling relentlessly to the plant.

Mme Alfred Carrière: one of the best climbers, palest pink to white, flowering early and late, even on a north wall.

Moyesii: a remarkable warm deep pink single rose with handsome flask-shaped hips. It can be seen growing against walls at Sissinghurst in Kent, and Beningborough in Yorkshire.

It is unfair to exclude modern roses—they do have the advantage of a long flowering season, and some are scented.

Crimson Glory: its name says all, except that it is a climber.

Mme Butterfly: another climber, pale pink and fragrant.

Fragrant Cloud: a hearty reddish-orange, but with a good scent.

Frau Karl Drushki: a lovely white, scentless, sadly.

Magenta: a modern 'old' rose, of a colour to blend well with the old roses, scented, and repeat flowering.

Guinée: a beautiful dark red with almost black shading, and scented. A climber.

Lady Hillingdon: comes either as a shrub or as a climber, and is an apricot-yellow, scented, repeat flowering rose which likes a warm wall.

Try combining one or two herbaceous clematis with your old roses: Edward Prichard has a scented pale lavender flower, Wyevale has blue bell-like flowers and is later than the other clematis, and Clematis recta has small white flowers. Feed both roses and clematis with well rotted compost or manure.

28

Scented Geraniums

These make good house and garden plants; the dried leaves can be added to all sorts of pot pourris and sachets (see pages 96–9), the fresh leaves give flavour to jams, jellies, cakes and syllabubs. The leaves themselves are more attractive than the flowers, which are often insignificant.

G. capitatum	— spicy lemon scent
G. citronella	— strongly lemon scented
G. crispum variegatum	— lemony and very decorative
G. denticulatum	— balsam scent, better for pot pourri
G. dichondraefolium	— lavender
G. fragrans	— pine
G. graveolens	— orange
G. Mons Ninon	— a rosy scent to add to jams
G. tomentosum	— peppermint
G. odoratissimum	— apple, rather like sweet briar leaves

For stockists, see the list at the end of the chapter. Geraniums strike easily and like hard pruning, but need to be brought indoors in the winter.

Bring flowering shrubs into the house while still tightly in bud, cutting small branches, hammering the stems, and standing them in warm water. Standing them in an airing cupboard will make them open earlier still.

To keep cut flowers fresh, cut and split the stalks a little every day, or as often as possible.

Add a pinch of salt and soda to the water. Or make an infusion of foxglove leaves, and add it to the water in the vases.

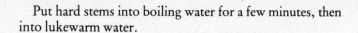

Put hard stems into boiling water for a few minutes, then into lukewarm water.

To make a Tussie-Mussie

These tightly packed aromatic nosegays of herbs and flowers were carried against the plague and unpleasant smells, and make a much nicer present for someone in hospital than a bunch of limp hothouse flowers. Take a good 'centre' flower, a moss rose-bud, a double pink, or something similar. Surround this with feathery leaves, artemisia, or sweet briar, and bind tightly with *wool*. Add thyme or marjoram flowers and bind again; encircle these with lavender, or rosemary, or eau de cologne mint alternating with pinks or more small rose-buds; bind again with wool and finally make a 'ruff' of stiff leaves such as bay, lambs' ears, box, etc, and finish with a final binding of wool. The point of the wool is that it will absorb water when the bunch is put in a vase, and will keep damp, and the flowers fresh, while they are being carried. Spring flowers are equally suitable—ivy makes a good collar for these, or you can use a paper doyley for a particularly Victorian effect. A winter version can be composed of the seed heads of Jerusalem sage, golden box, rosemary, artemisia, finished with a ruff of bay and elaeagnus leaves.

Bulbs

Bulb catalogues offer a bewildering array, and it is sometimes difficult to pick one's way through the 'bigger and better' varieties to the 'smaller and prettier' ones familiar to our grandparents and in danger of being forgotten. Here is a list of some of these:

Tulips
  Marjoletti, turkestanica, clusiana—or any of these small
    species tulips.
  Apricot Beauty, La Tulipe Noire (Queen of the Night),
    both singles.
  Snowstorm, Jewel Dance and Marechal Niel, all doubles.
  Hybrid 'Purissima', a most beautiful late-flowering white.
  Any of the Rembrandt, peony-flowered, parrot and
    fringed tulips, to create arrangements like the Dutch
    flower paintings.

Daffodils and narcissi
  Broughshane, Mount Hood, Empress of Ireland,
    Desdemona, Louise de Coligny (this last is scented).
  Albus plenus odoratus, telamonius plenus, Jenny, Dove
    Wings, W P Milner, the Tenby daffodil, the Lent Lily
    (or wild English daffodil), Old Pheasant Eye (unsur-
    passable scent).

Hyacinths
  Lady Derby, Ben Nevis, and all the small flowered
    cynthella and Roman hyacinths.

Miscellaneous bulbs and corms
  Anemone blanda, especially atrocoerulea; Chionodoxa
  (sardensis seems the best blue); cyclamen, the autumn and
  winter flowering winter varieties such as neapolitanum
  and repandum; erythronium, revolutum White Beauty;
  grape hyacinths, especially the white, scented *botryoides
  album*; fritillaries—meleagris for naturalising, and the
  old Imperial fritillary, prolifera, for the border; lilies,
  of which there are numerous sophisticated varieties, but I
  am fondest of the simplest, the Madonna lily and the
  martagons, both pink and white, which naturalise happily
  without attention; iris—reticulata, danfordiae, vartanii
  alba, magnifica, and the prolific Siberian irises in all their
  shades of blue and white.

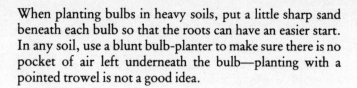

When planting bulbs in heavy soils, put a little sharp sand beneath each bulb so that the roots can have an easier start. In any soil, use a blunt bulb-planter to make sure there is no pocket of air left underneath the bulb—planting with a pointed trowel is not a good idea.

A guide to depth when planting is to measure the bulb from shoulder to base, then plant at twice this measurement, or slightly deeper in light soils. Crocus prefer shallow planting.

Hybrid tulips deteriorate after about two years, so cut off the dead heads and leave the foliage to die back (mark the place with a stick, if they are planted among other things). When the leaves are quite dead, lift the bulbs, dry off in the sun for two or three days, then put them into labelled brown paper bags. Store in a dry shed and replant in the early autumn.

Divide daffodil clumps in summer when the leaves have died back, but divide snowdrops as soon as they have finished flowering.

Dead-head all bulbs assiduously, and don't tie daffodil leaves into ugly knots—moisture from the leaves feeds the bulb ready for the next flowering season.

It is the practice in Holland to take up the Bulbs three weeks after bloom or when the leaves put on a yellowish appearance—cut the stems about an inch from the root but leave the fibres—place the bulbs in the same bed sideways, with their points towards the north, cover them half an inch deep with dry earth or sand—in the form of a ridge over each. Let them remain thus three weeks—admitting as much air as possible but keeping off heavy rain and too hot a sun. At the expiration of this period the bulbs are taken up and their fibres *gently* rubbed off—then place them in a dry room for a few days, and then clean away any soil that adheres to them, and their loose skins may be taken off. When this is finished the Bulbs are wrapped in separate pieces of paper or buried in dry sand until the return of the Season for planting.

Thomas Mawe and John Abercrombie, 1829

Early crocuses for the house: dig up the bulbs in the autumn and leave *on top* of the soil until January. Put in a bowl of bulb fibre mixed with light soil and keep moist, in the dark, for ten days, then bring into a warm, sunny room. Then when the flowers are over cut them off and allow the leaves to die back, while keeping the soil moist. When the leaves are dead, plant the bulbs back into the garden; allow two seasons' rest before forcing again.

Drying Flowers

By Silica Gel
This is obtainable from chemists and a fine grade is needed— no 22 is the most suitable. You will also need a shallow wooden box, such as a tomato or peach crate, a deeper cardboard box, clean sand, paraffin wax, cellulose filler and bicarbonate of soda. Fill in the cracks of the box with a cellulose filler, then drill holes along the slats to take the flower stalks. Stand the box over the cardboard box and arrange the flowers to be dried with their stalks through the holes in the slats, their heads flat on the wood. Heat about

33

8 lbs of sand in a low oven and mix with a tablespoon or two of melted paraffin wax—stir thoroughly, then add 8 oz silica gel and a dessertspoon of bicarbonate of soda. Sift this mixture lightly over, under and around the flower heads until they are completely covered, preserving the shape as carefully as possible. Roses, dahlias, pinks, carnations, etc, will only take about 48 hours, 'dense' flowers such as camellias may take a week. When the flowers are ready, remove, dust them with a paint-brush, arrange them, then spray with a pastel fixative. The silica/sand mixture can be dried out in a low oven and re-used many times.

Dried Flower and Seed-Head Arrangements

Seed-heads	Flowers
Love-in-a-mist	Mullein
Leeks	Helichrysum
Opium poppy	Delphinium
Foxglove	Helipterum
Lupin	Molucella
Grape hyacinth	Rhodanthe
Rudbekia	Statice
Hogweed	Sea lavender
Chives	Anaphalis
Fennel	Golden rod
Globe thistle	Achillea
Sea holly	Hops
Clematis	Clary
Ornamental grasses	Thrift
Allium montanum	Elecampane
Aquilegia	Lavender
Buddleia	Larkspur
Jerusalem sage	Globe artichoke
Jacob's ladder	

Hang all these plants upside down in a dry, airy place, such as a garage or barn. When larkspur, delphinium and other flowers with delicate petals are *almost* dry, take them down and stand each spike up in a bottle, smoothing the petals from time to time, until they are completely dry. Then tie the stems together, but not too many in any one bunch; if they are too closely packed, they may become mouldy in the middle, especially if the season is a wet one.

Seed pods that fluff up, such as golden rod, clematis, willow-herb etc, should be cut when immature, to prevent dropping.

Yarrow and achillea can be dipped in boracic powder before being hung up to dry, to preserve the colour.

To preserve ferns to remain green, pick them in midsummer and press them between sheets of newspaper under the carpet for about two months. To preserve other foliage green, pick before mid-summer, while the sap is still rising. Crush the stems and stand them in a mixture of 1 part glycerine to 2 parts water, boiled together briefly to mix them, then cooled. Pour about 2'' into a jamjar and stand the branches in this until drops appear on the leaves; wipe the leaves, then arrange them in a dry container.

For autumn colour, pick the leaves just as they are turning, stand them in the glycerine mixture, and proceed as above.

Miscellaneous Tips

To support herbaceous plants, place 12'' squares of large-mesh wire-netting over the young shoots of the plants and leave them to grow through, until about a foot high. Then push bamboo sticks through the netting to give further support.

Plant dahlias and their supportive stakes at the same time, to avoid damaging the tubers.

If you have an unmanageably large area of lawn, try allowing it to grow long in the summer, sowing a wild flower mixture suitable to your soil. Mow paths through it as it grows so that you can cross it without flattening the grasses and flowers. When all the flowers have seeded, scythe the area (the hay is very useful for pets), then mow. NB. This is *not* recommended for hay-fever sufferers.

Lawn sand: mix ½lb sulphate of iron with 1½lbs of sulphate of ammonia, and add this to 12 lbs of sand. Scatter over the lawn at the rate of 3 oz per square yard. A good general tonic.

An invaluable tip for June: 'Earwigs are now very trouble-some, and should be entrapped upon lobsters' claws stuck upon sticks.'

J H Clarke, c1850

I wonder how many cottagers had access to lobsters.

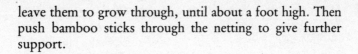

✎ *The Vegetable Garden* ✎

The average cottager grew subsistence crops only: potatoes, onions and cabbages. Peas, beans and lettuces were regarded as luxuries, like flowers, to be grown only when there was enough space, although small items such as radishes would be fitted in as 'relishes' for a diet of bread and cheese.

If the allotment was large enough, corn might be grown, harvested and threshed by hand and ground in the village mill. The straw would be used as litter for the cottager's pig, and this would be returned to the ground in the form of manure—recycling at its most efficient.

Hints on Growing

Nearly all root vegetables prefer ground which has been manured for a previous crop, as fresh manure produces forked roots in carrots and parsnips. Turnips and swedes are the exceptions and the ideal conditions for them are sandy soil and well-rotted cow or pig manure, plus a little lime.

Turnips in particular benefit from a sprinkling of super-phosphate or bonemeal in the drills before sowing, with the addition, if possible, of a little wood ash and soot to provide the vital diet of phosphate, potash and nitrogen.

Beetroot grow better on ground previously occupied by celery or leeks. The long varieties, such as Housewives' Choice, keep better than the round ones.

However large or small your garden, always plant your rows on a north-south axis, to make the most of the sun.

Stake brassicas in winter if your soil is light: it really does make a great deal of difference to the growth, particularly of sprouts. If you have firm soil, then firm planting, with occasional earthing up, especially after a frost, should be enough.

Globe artichokes are among my favourite herbaceous vegetables. They look splendid in the border, needing only a little manure and a little protection in the winter to produce delicious artichokes and beautiful flowers. Disbud from time to time to develop larger heads for eating, and allow the disbudded heads to open in water. When they are fully open, displaying blue thistly flowers, hang them up to dry.

Sea kale is another suitable subject for borders. Blanched in early spring, the shoots are one of the most delicate vegetables in the calendar; later on, when the plant has grown on, the large grey-green leaves and beautiful white sprays of flowers make it worthy of a place among flowers rather than vegetables (as *crambe maritima* it can be seen in the White Garden at Sissinghurst). It can be grown from seed quite easily.

The young Shoots of Salsifie will now [May] be fit to cut, and they are by many esteem'd very delicate eaten in the Manner of Asparagus: Hop tops make another Dish of the same Kind, and they are so wholesome as well as pleasant, that it is very well worth while to plant some Roots of the Hop about Hedges, or in other Places where as they grow up they will have Means of climbing.

John Hill, 1757

Turnip Stalks: take their Stalks (when they begin to run up to seed) as far as they will easily break downwards: Peel and tie them in Bundles. Then boiling them as they do Sparagus are to be eaten with melted Butter.

Acetaria

Asparagus should not be cut until its fourth season, so buy mature crowns if you are impatient. Stop cutting by mid-June and allow the fern to grow up; remove all the stems with berries, otherwise leave all the fern to go yellow.

Auspicious Days for Planting

Never plant during an eclipse, when everything in the garden was thought to stand still.

In Lancashire, St Gregory's Day (12 March) was considered the right day for onion setting.

Good Friday has always been regarded as a good day for planting anything from parsley to potatoes, probably because it was one of the few holidays an agricultural labourer had, although one among many explanations was that it was the day 'that Master's body was in the ground'. Flowering plants planted at noon on that day produced double flowers.

In Cheshire, potatoes were set on St Patrick's Day, 17 March. In both Buckinghamshire and Somerset, St Thomas's Day, 21 December, was the day for planting shallots and broad beans, as the days lengthened thereafter.

Potatoes

Nearly all the old varieties of potatoes grown before the First World War have disappeared, although one or two growers keep examples as museum pieces, like the wonderful 'forty-fold' potato so beloved of Mr Iden in Richard Jeffries' novel, *Amaryllis at the Fair*. Our favourites are Maris Piper, for flavour and keeping qualities, and a texture floury enough to make good mashed, boiled and roast potatoes, without 'boiling to a smash', and Aura, a waxy potato for salads; it seems a pity that while we are expected to eat Golden Delicious apples from France, the best of their salad potatoes make all too rare an appearance.

The Gardener's Chronicle in 1849 advised removing the flowers from potato plants as soon as they appeared to increase the yield, and to keep the plants green so that they could be used as a green manure after the tubers had been harvested.

Put small new potatoes in a dry biscuit tin and cover with dry sand; seal the tin well with sticky tape and bury in the garden. Do not dig it up until Christmas. The potatoes will taste as good as they did in early summer. Mark the spot carefully.

A Lancashire hot-pot for lean days: layer potatoes, tapioca, carrots, split peas and onions with plenty of seasoning, and add water to come to the top layer (which should be of potatoes). Cook this very slowly—it would have cooked in a cooling bread oven or on the back of a stove—and serve it very hot with plenty of good crusty bread. I also make this with pearl barley, as tapioca is not to everyone's taste.

Boiled potatoes: scrub a panful of King Edward potatoes and cover them with cold water. Add plenty of salt, and bring to the boil. Cook rapidly until the potatoes are only just tender, then drain them well and return to the pan over a very low heat. Put a clean, folded tea-towel over the pan and continue to cook them thus until the skins split.

Pile them on to a hot dish, without covering, and serve at once, with lots of unsalted butter. This is as nutritious a dish as anyone could wish for, and one which kept most farm labourers alive and fairly well for two centuries, although the butter would have been replaced by rosemary-flavoured lard from their own pig.

Onions

Prepare an onion bed by forking in 4 oz of wood ash and 2 oz old soot to every square yard.

> Onion skin very thin
> Mild winter coming in.
> Onion skin thick and tough
> Winter weather cold and rough.

Try growing the new varieties of Japanese onion for an early crop; sow in August and they will be ready to lift by the following June. They are mild and sweet enough to be added raw to salads, or to be cooked as follows:

To Boil Onions (From Mr Gordon)
Take the largest Onions; when you have cut off the Strings of the Roots, and the green Tops, without taking off any of the Skins, fling them into Salt and Water, and let them lie an Hour, then wash them in it, and put them into a Kettle,

where they may have Plenty of Water, and boil them till they are tender, then take them off; and take off as many Skins as you think fit, till you come to the white Part, then bruise them, and toss them up with a little Cream or Milk and Butter.

Richard Bradley, 1753

To make plaits of onions, garlic or shallots: knot together firmly 3 pieces of string or raffia, about 2″ long.

Arrange the strings with the ends nearest you and take 3 onions, twisting the withered stems round the strings, then plait these tightly twice, repeat with another set of 3, and continue until the string is used up, leaving enough to bind the ends together. All these vegetables are best stored in an airy place, such as a cool larder or outhouse rather than a steamy kitchen, so the plaits are not simply decorative, but practical, too.

Cabbage

Sow spring cabbage in late July and plant out in the autumn into unmanured ground.

Sow both winter and summer cabbages in March, and sow winter cabbage again in early May for a succession.

For cabbage root fly, treat the plants with calomel dust when planting; this also helps with club root (lime the soil and the seed beds as a further precaution against the latter).

Peas and Beans

When sowing peas allow the height of the peas plus 1''
between the rows—if your garden is small either sow 1 long
row, or grow the dwarf varieties such as Little Marvel or
Rent-payer.

Sow 2 peas or beans in each hole, and transplant the extra
seedlings to fill in any gaps in the rows.

In dry weather, soak the earth around peas and beans with
plenty of water from the hose, then mulch thickly with a
mixture of grass mowings and poultry droppings.

Saving seeds of peas and beans for planting—select one or
two of the best plants early in the season and do not pick the
pods, but leave them on the plants until almost dry and the
seeds firm and tough. Pick the plants and hang them, pods
and all, in a dry and airy place. When quite dry, shuck the
seeds and store them in dark glass jars or brown paper bags,
labelling clearly.

A Green-bean Pudding

Boil and blanch old beans, beat them in a mortar with *very*
little pepper and salt, some cream, and the yolk of an egg. A
little spinach-juice will give a finer colour, but it is good
without. Boil it in a basin that will just hold it, an hour; and
pour parsley and butter over. Serve bacon to eat with it.

Mrs Rundell, 1818

This is a delicious recipe for old broad beans, which need the
tough outer skins removed in any case.

🌿 *The Fruit Garden* 🌿

The best situation for an orchard or fruit garden is a gentle slope towards the South, South-East, or East—with regard to soil, good corn land is said to do well for fruit; good loam is best.

Elizabeth Watts, c1885

As a rough guide to fruit growing—a medium soil will grow anything; a heavy soil will not grow cherries, but is good for quinces, medlars, loganberries and blackberries; a chalk soil is good for plums and cherries.

July 13. Mackay, Gardner at Norwich, called here this Even', and he walked over my garden with me—He told me how to preserve my Fruit Trees etc from being injured for the future by the ants, which was to wash them well with soap sudds after our general washing, especially in the winter.

The Rev James Woodforde, 1781

Fruit gathered too timely will taste of the wood
Will shrink and be bitter and seldom prove good:
So fruit that is shaken, and beat off a tree,
With bruising in falling, soon faulty will be

Thomas Tusser, 1573

Fruit trees in the West Country were 'wassailed' at New Year to encourage good crops for cider and perry; cider was thrown up into the branches, and cider and perry soaked toast was left out 'for the orchard gods'.

44

Apples

The Irish Peach-apple is the best-flavoured early apple we have; white in the flesh, tender, rich, juicy, and high-flavoured. It is a very bright-coloured, beautiful-looking apple.

Elizabeth Watts, c1885

With the proliferation of apples grown for their commercial qualities rather than those of flavour and texture, it would seem as important to conserve old apples as it is to preserve old vegetables, wild flowers and animals. A visit to New England last October impressed on us the American love and knowledge of good apples; they are sold along main roads from wayside stalls manned by helpful people who gave us tastings and explained the relative merits of each apple. It re-kindled my enthusiasm for good apples and on my return I set about discovering how many of the favourite old varieties were still available. With a pile of old gardening books at one hand and of new gardening catalogues at the other, I found that many could still be bought. Here is my short list, based on Scotts' excellent catalogue (for the address, see the end of this chapter):

Eating apples
  Early: Beauty of Bath, with Irish Peach to pollinate. These should be picked and eaten as quickly as possible.
  Mid-season: Egremont Russet, King of the Pippins, Margil to pollinate. Of King of the Pippins, Mrs Watts writes— 'flesh is yellow-white, firm, crisp, juicy, sweet, and full-flavoured. It is a handsome apple, nice for eating in November and December, and the tree is hardy and a good bearer.'

45

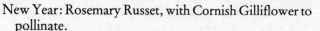

New Year: Rosemary Russet, with Cornish Gilliflower to
pollinate.

Other varieties to try: D'Arcy Spice, Pitmaston Pineapple,
Cornish Aromatic. Some of these are not as impervious
to blight as modern varieties, some are light croppers,
but all make up for this in flavour.

Cooking apples

Early: Golden Noble, Peasgood's Nonesuch (Mrs Watts
again: 'Golden Noble—bakes to a soft, amber-coloured
pulp, with a fine rich flavour, and just acidity enough.')

Late: Annie Elizabeth, Wellington.

Crab apples are also worth growing for looks as well as fruit;
Dartmouth has scented white flowers followed by crimson
fruit in October which makes a delicious jelly. John Downie
has equally useful fruit, this time yellow flushed with scarlet,
ripening rather earlier than Dartmouth.

Try baking Golden Noble apples in foil in the ashes of a
wood fire, scooping out the core and adding a good lump of
unsalted butter and a spoonful of brown sugar, before eating
with a spoon, as if it were a boiled egg.

Apples prefer a slightly damp atmosphere for storage, so a
cellar is ideal; pears prefer it warm and dry, so use the attic.

Apples can be wrapped in waxed paper if space is limited for
storage, but a ventilated apple rack, or slatted shelves, is
better, as the apples can more easily be checked for signs of
rot. Make sure they do not touch.

46

Windfall apples can be used in several ways: in jellies and chutneys, as bottled or frozen purée, or for drying.

To dry apples: peel and core the apples, cut out any bad bits, then slice into rings about ¼″ thick. As you slice the apples, put them into a large bowl of water to which you have added the juice of a lemon, to keep the slices from going brown.

Thread the rings either on to string, or on clean bamboo canes, to hang over a central-heating boiler or solid-fuel cooker; or arrange them in single layers on baking trays and dry in a cool oven (80°C, 160°F). The rings, when dry, should look and feel like chamois leather. Leave for 24 hours before storing in airtight jars; soak for at least 24 hours before use. They can be used in a winter fruit salad.

Apple purée for freezing or bottling: do not peel or core the apples, but simply cut out any bruised or bad bits, then cut the fruit into rough chunks. Put about ½″ cider in a heavy pan, add the apples, and cook gently, stirring from time to time, until the fruit is soft and fluffy. Put through a sieve or food-mill, then either freeze or bottle; I keep my purée unseasoned so that I can use it for sweet or savoury purposes.

Elderberries are a very good addition to many apple dishes, especially in a poor blackberry year; try baked apples stuffed with them, apple pie with a tablespoon or two of them, or apple sauce for pork seasoned with them.

Pears

Pears are more temperamental than apples, preferring sun and shelter. They produce leaves and blossom early in the season which makes them particularly susceptible to damage

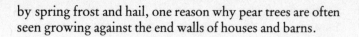

by spring frost and hail, one reason why pear trees are often seen growing against the end walls of houses and barns.

Elizabeth Watts recommends Williams' Bon-Chrétien, 'large and handsome, juicy and sweet', with 'a musky flavour'. 'Winter Nelis is a pear which no garden should be without. It is a mellow, delicious, sweet, juicy pear, with a rich, fine flavour.' 'Joséphine de Malines—has a peculiar hyacinth-like scent; The pear is rich, sweet, and juicy, with a very fine aroma.'

Williams' Bon-Chrétien is an early pear, while both Winter Nelis and Joséphine de Malines are December ripening. For a summer pear, Jargonelle is a very old variety of high quality, which does well in the north.

In Worcestershire, superstition dictates that last year's brew of perry is not opened until the next season's blossom has appeared.

Quince

The Quince is also, for itself, a fruit worth cultivating, if room can be spared for a tree, because stewed quinces are really very delicious, much finer than any stewed pears, and for cooking in different ways, and for marmalade, they are good.

Elizabeth Watts, c1885

Champion is a good apple-shaped variety of quince; Mrs Watts recommends it (by type, not name) as 'very superior in flavour and appearance'. It has beautiful large white flowers, and huge fresh green leaves, silver-backed. On the right deep rich soil, quinces can grow up to eighteen feet, although most remain about twelve. All varieties are self-fertile, and will crop after about five years, but as the tree is attractive anyway, the delay is bearable.

Japonica (or cydonia) fruit is a variety of quince and makes very good jelly, particularly when mixed with apples. *Cydonia maulei*, or Chinese quince, is a neat round bush, only about two feet high, with pale coppery flowers and large golden fruit—a good dual purpose shrub for a small garden.

Plums and Damsons

Cooking Plums: Belle de Louvain, Warwickshire Drooper, Wyedale, Rivers Early Prolific.
Dessert: Count Althann's Gage, Kirke's Blue, Washington.
Damson: Shropshire Prune—a light cropper, but with outstanding flavour.
Gages: Early and Late Transparent, Old Greengage (this last is a very light cropper in the north, but with an incomparable honey flavour).

All the above plums do best 'in counties furthest from the Atlantic'. Certainly our Cumbrian plum crop is at best erratic, very heavy in a good year, non-existent in a poor one, although Kendal damsons are famous. The cherry plum, or myrobolan, another decorative tree, is more vigorous; the fruit is very good for bottling and preserving in brandy (see page 77).

Cherries

Cherries can be grown in the south and east where the climate is warm and dry with no danger of late frosts. It can be an advantage to grow them against a wall, where they can be netted to protect the fruit from birds; when grown in an orchard they become tall very fast—up to thirty feet in height.

Morello Wine

Take 24 lbs of Morello Cherries, pull off the stalkes, and bruise them so that the stones may be broken, press out the juice and put it to 10 gallons of White-wine. Put the skins and the stones in a Bag and let them be hung in a Cask so as not to touch the bottom of it and let it stand for a month or more. You may also put in spices if you please but the wine will be very pleasant without them.

John Nott, 1723

Soft Fruit

If you live in a good area for pick-your-own fruit, it is debatable whether it is worth troubling to grow much soft fruit; most of it needs netting, and strawberries in particular need space. We grow wild strawberries, white and red, as ground cover—they do cover too much ground if left un-checked, and are fiddly to pick, but are so pretty and so delicious that these nuisances are willingly tolerated. Red, white and black currants, and gooseberries, are all useful; white currants in particular make a good dessert fruit if left on the bushes until ripe-to-bursting.

To top and tail gooseberries the modern way, freeze the fruit, and while still frozen, rub them in a rough towel—the tops and tails will come off easily.

June 23—Dessert after dinner a vast profusion of Strawberries of 5 different sorts—The Scarlet, the Chili, the Hautboy, the Alpine and the White Wood. We did not get home till 10 o'clock.

The Rev James Woodforde, c1790

Blackcurrant Leaf Syllabub

Infuse a large handful of young blackcurrant leaves in ½ pint white wine, heated to boiling point; strain when the flavour is strong enough and stir in 3 oz of caster sugar until it has dissolved. Cool, then fold in ½ pint whipped cream. Serve in little cups decorated with small currant leaves.

Blackcurrant Wine

To every 3 quarts of juice allow the same amount of water unboiled, and to every 3 quarts of the liquid add 3 lbs very pure moist sugar. Put all into a Cask, reserving a little for filling up: Place the cask in a warm, dry room, the liquid will ferment of itself. Skim off the refuse when fermentation ceases, fill up with the reserved liquid when it has ceased working, pour in 3 quarts of brandy to 4 quarts wine. Bung it close for 9 months, then bottle it and strain the thick part through a Jelly bag, when it also can be bottled. Keep 10 or 12 months before drinking.

Travels Round Our Village

The raspberry cane so loves moisture and richness combined that some growers have found them thrive best planted in trenches a yard wide and eighteen inches deep, like celery trenches, manuring the surface from time to time; to retain the damp of the summer rains.

Elizabeth Watts, c1885

Late pruning of raspberries (in September) will give a later crop, but this is not advisable in an area of early frosts.

🍃 *General Gardening Hints* 🍃

Compost and Manure

Layer vegetable and flower waste, and biodegradable kitchen rubbish with a scattering of soil mixed with lime, every 12". Continue until the compost heap comes to within about 6" of the top, cover with 6" of soil and a lid of sacking, old carpet, or polythene. Keep the rain out, the heat in, and let the heap breathe.

Dead leaves are best piled into their own enclosure of wire-netting (held rigid by bamboo poles at intervals), and left to rot down to leaf mould, rather than added to the general compost heap.

Liquid Manure

Fill a large barrel with fresh cow dung or horse droppings, cover well and leave for at least three weeks. Add a trowelful of this to a gallon of rainwater for a very strong brew, or dilute a pint of the first dilution with another gallon of

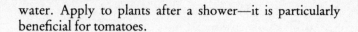

water. Apply to plants after a shower—it is particularly beneficial for tomatoes.

> Lime, lime, and no manure
> Makes the father rich and the son poor.

A heavily manured garden may still lack lime—apply it on or near the surface of the soil some time before any other fertilisers are used.

Use cow or pig manure on light soils, horse manure to lighten heavy soils. Cover a fresh manure heap while it rots down to prevent evaporation, and dilution by rain.

Bonfire ash is valuable where potash is needed, to add to potting composts and to use as a mulch mixed with grass mowings.

Green manuring: all the leguminous plants have roots rich in nitrogen—a crop of annual lupins, or vetch, or mustard, or clover, sown over an area of poor soil and dug in just before they flower, will provide both nitrogen and humus.

Potting Composts

For seed boxes: mix 2 parts sieved soil, 1 part sharp sand, 1 part peat or sieved leaf mould with a sprinkling of bonfire ash and spent hops.
For potting-up: 5 parts sieved soil, 2 parts sieved compost, 1 part sand.

Either of these mixtures can be used, with advantage, to line seed drills before sowing.

Any gardening bits and pieces, such as plant labels, ties, slug pellets, etc, which can be stored in jamjars, can be kept underneath a shelf, by nailing the screw-tops to the underside of the shelf and screwing the jars up into the lids. This leaves the top of the shelf free for other oddments.

To Clean Greened Greenhouse or Conservatory Glass
Mix 2 teaspoons of ammonia with a pint of paraffin, and wipe this mixture over the dirty glass. Leave for 24 hours, then polish it off with a clean cloth.

Cuttings

You are supposed to take hard-wood cuttings in autumn and soft-wood cuttings in spring, but if you keep a cutting bed in a sheltered corner of the garden, you can take cuttings at almost any time of year; mix plenty of sand into the soil, and keep the leaves moist in dry weather. Hormone rooting powder is necessary for plants which do not strike readily, like azaleas, kalmias and viburnums, or you can try the old trick of inserting a grain of wheat into a slit cut in the base of the stalk, which encourages rooting.

Berried shrubs can be grown from seed very easily, or you can often find seedlings which have sprouted in odd corners of the garden from seed dropped by birds; don't throw these on the compost heap, but pot them up and give them to friends, or sell them at fêtes.

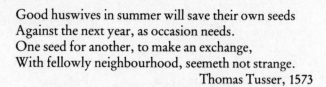

Good huswives in summer will save their own seeds
Against the next year, as occasion needs.
One seed for another, to make an exchange,
With fellowly neighbourhood, seemeth not strange.

Thomas Tusser, 1573

Hand Care

When weeding or planting out, protect your hands by
wearing a pair of old fabric gloves with the tips of the fingers
cut off; scrape your nails on a bar of soap to keep earth from
working its way under them. Fabric gloves are preferable to
rubber ones, which are both clumsy and sweaty.

If you prefer, make a barrier lotion by mixing equal quantities
of glycerine, lemon juice and eau de cologne. Apply gener-
ously before gardening, and wash off afterwards—the dirt
will come off easily.

To clean already stained hands, mix 2 teaspoons of ammonia
with ¼ pint rainwater and 3 fl oz glycerine and use before
washing.

Charles Carter offers a more ladylike recipe:
To clean and soften the Hands—Take four Ounces of
blanch'd Almonds beaten fine into a quart of Milk; as soon
as it begins to boil take it off, and thicken it with a couple of
Yolks of Eggs, set it on the Fire again, add two small
spoonfuls of Oil, and put it up in a Gallipot for use. A Bit of
this about the Bigness of a Walnut rubbed about the Hands,
the Dirt will rub off and it will render them very soft and

smooth. If one Person only be to use it, half the quantity may suffice to be made at once, for it will not hold good above a week.

It can be stored in the fridge, carefully labelled as it is also good as a salad-dressing.

Plant Suppliers

Jaques Amand, Beethoven Street, London W10 4LG (bulbs).

David Austin, Bowling Green Lane, Albrighton, Wolverhampton WV7 3HB (roses).

Walter Blom & Son Ltd, Leavesden, Watford, Herts WD2 7BH (bulbs).

Beth Chatto, White Barn House, Elmstead Market, Colchester, Essex (unusual plants).

Fibrex Nurseries, Harvey Road, Evesham, Worcestershire (scented geraniums).

Great Dixter Nurseries, Northiam, Sussex (clematis, especially).

Intwood Nurseries, Swardeston, Norwich (roses).

Scotts Nurseries, Merriott, Somerset (roses, shrubs and old varieties of fruit trees).

van Tubergen, Willowbank Wharf, Ranelagh Gardens, London SW6 3JY (bulbs).

Wallace & Barr, The Nurseries, Marden, Kent TN12 9BP (bulbs).

🍃 *Country Housekeeping* 🍃

There are few more enjoyable ways of helping the family economy than by cutting lavender on a warm July day, to make up into lavender bags which will scent your sheets and towels for the next year, or by picking fruit in your own garden, to turn into jams, jellies, chutneys, wines and cordials. I have not yet made my own linen from the flax I grow as an edging plant, nor have I yet persuaded my family to let me have a pig, although my husband is indefatigable in seeking out supplies of 'antique' pigs for the freezer (so much nicer than those over-lean and tasteless modern breeds). We do grow most of our own herbs, although some are difficult in the north, and I do try a herbal cure for something before telephoning the doctor or the vet.

Country Housekeeping can be enjoyed on any level, whether it is total self-sufficiency, or simply growing a few lettuces in a tiny cottage garden. Filling the larder shelves with preserves and wines is rather more pleasurable than filling the freezer, I find, although I try to do both. Somehow the freezer has little aesthetic appeal, although it is useful for storing raw ingredients and if I do not have time for making jam when the fruit is ready, then it can be picked and frozen until I have. Even Seville oranges freeze well, so you can make your marmalade as and when required; I learnt only last winter how delicious marmalade is when eaten fresh, within a month or so of being made. I had always left it to mature before, but shall do so no longer.

The few recipes I include in the first part of this chapter have little to do with the modern preoccupations of heart and figure, but a great deal to do with the old necessities of keeping the body and soul firmly together. The Old Country Housewife knew, without putting it into words, the values of calories in fuelling her family for hard manual labour and she often had to do this on a very restricted income. Dumplings are no bad way of filling up a crowd of hungry children on a winter's evening, now as then, and I have never known anyone refuse a helping of suet pudding, stuffed with apples and elderberries, or damsons, with lots of real custard poured over it. I used a crock-pot when testing recipes such as the ones on pages 60 and 61 for bread-oven chicken and hot-pot, having neither the cooling bread-oven nor the blackened range as required by the original recipes. I found it cooked everything slowly and carefully, making the best of the cheapest ingredients, and I can recommend it to all New Country Housewives who do not possess an Aga.

Country wines are magical ways of turning innocent ingredients into lethal beverages; I was told of bread wine, and toast wine, I saw bottles of tea wine and burnet wine bearing prize-winning rosettes at our local agricultural show only yesterday, and on a memorable weekend some years ago, we tasted carrot whisky and parsnip gin, elderberry port and potato rum. The parsley wine on page 90 is so light and delicate that only when we were shown the bottle did we believe it wasn't a very good German hock. The recipe for Gingerette on page 90 is not alcoholic, but its effect is as electric and much to be recommended when temperatures fall as low as they did in January '82. The medicines given are all quite safe and practical, although I doubt that many people will want to try the snail cure for consumption. Nonetheless, having just paid over a pound for a bottle of simple cough syrup, I shall henceforth put my researches into practice (safe in the knowledge that if they fail, our patient GP will set us back on the right path with a dose of penicillin).

❧ *The Kitchen* ☙

The clear bright fire, the whitened hearth, the yellow-ochred walls, the polished tins, the clean-scrubbed tables and chairs, and the white dresser cloths, of the kitchen, such as I have always been used to see at my own home.

Anne Cobbett, 1851

The picture this conjures up, for me, is principally one of the food cooked in such a kitchen—solid, comforting country dishes. In this section I give recipes for just this sort of food, before it disappears entirely in our cholesterol-conscious society. Here is Parson Woodforde's family dinner, 1792: July 30 Monday—Beans and Bacon, a blackbird Pudding, a Beef-Stake Pye cold, and a Couple of rost Chickens and pickled Mushroom and black and red Currant Pies.

Parsley Pie
This may be made of veal, fowl, or calf's feet, but the latter partley cooked first; scald a cullender full of fresh parsley in

milk, season it with salt, pepper and nutmeg, add a teaspoonful of broth, and pour it into a pie dish, over the meat. When baked, pour in ¼ pint of scalded cream.

Anne Cobbett, 1851

This recipe does have a lid of shortcrust pastry, although the method makes no mention of it. I make the pie from chicken, first blanched in water brought to the boil with salt and lemon added, then drained well. I thicken the milk in which I have scalded the parsley (about ¼ pint) with a little cornflour as this stops it from curdling. Bake the pie for 2 hours, at 400°F for the first 25 minutes to brown the pastry, then at 325°F for the rest of the time to cook the filling. It is also very good cold.

A Jugged Hare

Cut your Hare into small Pieces, season them with a little Pepper and Salt, put them into an Earthen Jugg, with a Blade or two of Mace, an Onion, and Sweet-herbs; cover the Jugg close, then set it in a Pot of boiling water, keep the water boiling, and three Hours will do it, then turn it out into the Dish, and send it to Table, without the Onion and Sweet-herbs.

Richard Bradley, 1753

This is genuine jugged hare, and worth trying—the narrowness of the jug means there is less surface evaporation, so the meat is steamed. An old hare will need almost 5 hours' cooking. (Sweet Herbs are bay-leaves, marjoram, parsley, sage and thyme.)

Bread-oven Chicken

An old East Anglian recipe where the chicken was put in to cook after the bread had come out of the oven. A crock-pot cooks it almost as well; put it in in the morning and come back to a hot supper.

A boiling fowl, about 4 lbs	Salt and pepper
1 pint milk	4 oz brown rice
3 small onions,	A blade of mace
each stuck with a clove	

Preheat the crock-pot on High. Cover the fowl with cold water to which you have added a good squeeze of lemon, bring it to the boil and then simmer for 10 minutes; drain it well (make sure there is no water left in the cavities) and put it in the pot. Bring the milk, onions, rice, mace, salt and pepper to the boil and pour immediately over the fowl. Put the lid on the pot and leave on the High setting for half-an-hour, before reducing it to Low for 8 hours. To serve, joint the chicken and arrange it on the rice; thicken the sauce if necessary, check for seasoning and pour it over the meat. Dust with chopped parsley.

Cottage Hot-pot

Almost everyone has their own version of this recipe, and it is possible to determine the social level of the household by the cuts of lamb used, and the additions suggested, from black pudding, through oysters to mushrooms and kidneys. However, this recipe is as 'pure' a version as I could find:

1½ lbs neck chops of lamb
1½ lbs potatoes, peeled and thickly sliced
½ lb onions, peeled and sliced
1 black pudding (about 12 oz)
Water
Salt and pepper

Simply layer the ingredients, seasoning as you do so, in a deep earthenware casserole with a well-fitting lid. Pour in water to come level with the top layer, which should be of potatoes. Cook this very slowly, all day, and eat it hot, on hot plates, with pickled red cabbage. If you make this in a crock-pot, simply put all the ingredients in a heavy pan and bring them to a brisk simmer before transferring them to the preheated pot; any harm done by this initial harsh treatment is corrected by the long slow cooking that follows.

Despite the simplicity of the ingredients, the flavour is excellent; more expensive cuts of lamb do not work nearly as well, and undoubtedly need the extra flavour supplied by oysters or mushrooms.

Uncle Henry's Onions

Very good as part of a ploughman's lunch of bread and cheese. Cut a large mild onion into thin slices and pour boiling water over it. Leave to cool, then drain and cover with vinegar. Leave overnight and eat next day.

Steaks and Ale

This next recipe has been claimed as 'local' by almost every county in England—I have found it called Staffordshire Beef Steaks, Lancashire Oven Beef and Sussex Stewed Steak. It is very simple to prepare.

    1½ lbs shoulder steak
    2 large onions
    1 bottle stout
    2 tblsps mushroom ketchup
    Salt and pepper

Slice the onions and put half of them in a shallow dish, season them lightly and put the steak flat on top; season again and cover with the remaining onions, mix the stout and ketchup and pour over. Make sure the lid fits well, then cook slowly for 2–3 hours, or all day if more convenient. The gravy is a wonderful dark brown, and the meat very tender. Serve with floury potatoes boiled in their skins (see page 40).

Shropshire Fitchett Pie

Make a pastry crust with 8 oz flour and 4 oz lard, salt and a little pepper. For the filling, peel and slice half a pound each of well-flavoured apples and potatoes; cut 6 oz of bacon into cubes, and slice a small onion. Mix these ingredients together in a pie dish, adding seasoning, and just enough stock to moisten it—the apples will provide more as they cook. Cover the dish with the pastry, leaving a vent for the steam to escape, decorate with pastry trimmings, brush with beaten egg and bake for 25 minutes in a hot (400°F) oven, then lower the heat to about 350°F and cook for another 1¼ hours. Serve either hot or cold.

Variations of this pie were made with lamb or mutton instead of bacon.

A country housewife may have a fisherman in the family who might bring home a catch worth cooking. For really fresh fish, the simplest ways are best.

Brown trout: out of the water, into the frying pan, to cook in plenty of butter for about 10 minutes each side, over a moderate heat. Or, poach them very gently in water to which you have added a glass of dry white wine or cider and a little salt. Serve with melted butter.

Rainbow trout: these have a little less flavour than the brown trout, even when spanking fresh, so wrap them in streaky bacon and bake them in the oven for about 25 minutes at 350°F for trout weighing about 8 oz.

Salmon and salmon trout: bake these in the oven at 325°F, wrapped in oiled foil and lightly seasoned, allowing about 25 minutes to the pound. If the fish are very large, cut into manageable joints (of which the tail joint is the most succulent), and freeze the rest. As with trout, simple melted butter is the best sauce, or a jug of hot thick cream to which you have added the juices from the cooked fish, and chopped parsley, tarragon and chives.

Grayling: fill the cavities with dried thyme and grill them, basting with a little butter to keep them moist.

Gudgeon: flour them lightly with seasoned flour, dip in egg and breadcrumbs, and fry in a mixture of butter and oil.

The only place where the English breakfast remains alive and well—apart from the transport cafés—is in the country, and then mainly on farms where a 5 am start means a roaring appetite by 8 o'clock. Our farm-worker neighbour comes back to cook himself a huge bacon-and-egg breakfast at about 9.30; the smell of frying bacon is one of the most appetising of all, and every day I have to resist the temptation to do the same. Here is a very old dish which deserves a revival as a good way of ekeing out expensive bacon; it is equally delicious for high tea.

Bacon Fraize

Cut streaky bacon into strips and fry them gently until just beginning to crisp. Pour into the pan enough pancake batter to cover the bottom of the pan, and when it is set, turn the pancake over and cook the other side.

This recipe is a wartime one and very useful as it can be made up the night before from left-overs:

Potato Sausages

Cook some finely chopped onion in a little well-flavoured dripping until soft, then mix well with cold mashed potato. Season well, and add a teaspoon of Marmite if you like. Form this mixture into sausages, flour them lightly, then dip in egg and breadcrumbs, and leave on a cake rack until the morning. Then fry them until crisp in more dripping, and serve them either on their own, or with bacon, eggs and pork sausages.

Breakfast can be made or marred by the bread.

White Bread

1½ lbs strong plain white flour
1 sachet Harvest Gold dried yeast
2 teasps salt
About ¾ pint lukewarm water

Mix the salt, yeast and flour well together, then add the water until you have a stiff dough. Knead until the dough is smooth and springy and leaves the bowl clean. Sprinkle more flour over the bottom of the bowl and leave the dough to rise, covered with a cloth, until doubled in size. Knead again and either shape into two rounds on a greased baking sheet, or fit into well-greased bread tins. Heat the oven to 425°F, put in the bread and bake for 15 minutes before lowering the heat to 350°F and baking for a further 30 minutes. The loaves are done when they sound hollow when tapped on the bottom. Cool them on a cake rack. I find this new 'instant' yeast, which requires no pre-mixing with water, works even better than the traditional baker's yeast, and with no loss of that wonderful yeasty taste.

65

To make yeast

Boil together 2 oz hops, 3 tablespoonfuls sugar, 4 pints water. Strain and leave to cool. Mix 2 tablespoonfuls flour with part of the liquid, add the remaining liquid and bottle, cork very firmly and leave to ferment (allow plenty of space in the bottle to prevent it bursting). Use 1 teaspoonful to 3 lbs flour.

Soda Bread

Delicious, and a useful standby when snowed in.

    1½ lbs wholemeal flour
    2 teasps salt
    1½ teasps bicarbonate of soda
    1½ teasps cream of tartar
    About ¾ pint warm milk and water mixed

Mix all the dry ingredients and add about ½ pint of the liquid; work to a dough which leaves the bowl clean, adding more liquid if necessary (flours vary enormously in their absorbency). Do not knead, or leave to rise, but shape into two flat buns, cut a deep cross in the centre of each, dust with a little of the wholemeal flour and bake on a greased baking sheet for 50 minutes at 400°F. Again, the bread is done when the base of the loaf sounds hollow when tapped. Cool on a cake rack. This bread is at its very best eaten warm, but it will keep a day or two, and is good toasted.

Rule-of-Egg Cake

    2 eggs, plus their weight in butter, caster sugar and
        self-raising flour
    4 rose or lemon scented geranium leaves

Weigh the eggs together (size 2 eggs weigh about 2¼ oz each), then weigh out the same amount of butter (or soft margarine), caster sugar and self-raising flour. Cream the butter and sugar, then add the eggs one at a time, each accompanied by a sprinkle of flour. Beat hard, then fold in the flour quickly and lightly and do not beat again. Divide the mixture between two greased and floured 8″ sandwich tins, and arrange 2 geranium leaves on top of each tin. Bake for 25 minutes in the centre of an oven heated to 375°F. Sandwich, when cool, with home-made jam (blackberry is particularly good), and dust the tops with caster sugar. Remove the leaves when the cake is lukewarm.

Gingerbread

½ lb self-raising flour	Saltspoon salt
½ lb wholemeal flour	1 lb golden syrup
8 oz margarine	3 tblsps marmalade
5 oz demerara sugar	½ pint milk
2 large eggs	2 teasps mixed spice
2 teasps ginger	1 teasp bicarbonate of soda

Line a loaf tin with greaseproof paper. Melt the margarine, syrup, sugar and marmalade together over a low heat, then leave to cool. Mix all the other dry ingredients; beat the eggs into the milk and stir this into the cooled syrup mixture, then into the dry ingredients to make the batter. Pour into the tin and bake at 325°F for 2¾ hours.

The following recipe is for an eighteenth-century gingerbread which was a flat spicy biscuit, more like a gingernut than the gingerbread with which we are familiar.

To make a good GINGERBREAD without Butter

Take two Pounds of Treacle, candied Orange, Lemon and Citron-peel, of each a quarter of a Pound; as much candied

Ginger, all sliced thin; one Ounce of Carraway-seed, and one Ounce of Coriander-seed, with one Ounce of beaten Ginger; mix in as much Flour as will make it a soft Paste; lay it in Cakes on Tin Plates, and bake it in a quick Oven; keep it dry and it will be good some Months.

Richard Bradley, 1753

Norfolk Rusks

1 lb flour	2 large eggs
2 teasps baking powder	Milk
6 oz butter	Pinch salt

Heat the oven to 450°F. Rub the butter into the flour until fine, with the baking powder and salt. Beat the eggs together a little, then add them to the dry mixture, adding a little milk if necessary to make a soft dough. Roll out to about ¾" thick and cut into rounds. Bake on a greased baking sheet for 10–15 minutes. Take them out of the oven and split them in half (don't cut them, make a cut with a sharp knife and then pull them apart), and return them to the oven split side up. Lower the heat to 350°F and bake until crisp and pale gold.

I am told the next recipe is a Shropshire delicacy, although I first had it in Staffordshire.

Elderberry Pudding

Line a two-pint pudding basin with a suet crust, keeping back some for the lid. Fill the centre with elderberries, strigged from their stalks, 2 peeled, cored and sliced cooking apples and 2 oz brown sugar. Pinch the lid on top, cover with greaseproof paper, then a cloth, and boil for 2½ hours. Turn out and serve with real custard.

What's for Tea in the Counties?

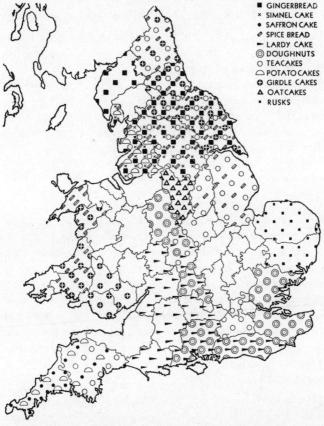

- ■ GINGERBREAD
- × SIMNEL CAKE
- ● SAFFRON CAKE
- ◆ SPICE BREAD
- ━ LARDY CAKE
- ◎ DOUGHNUTS
- ○ TEACAKES
- ◠ POTATO CAKES
- ✚ GIRDLE CAKES
- △ OATCAKES
- · RUSKS

This map was published in The Countryman *magazine in the autumn of 1947, and appears here with their kind permission. I wonder what such a map would reveal today? Unfortunately, there is no trace of the second map, for pies and pastries.*

Custard

2 large eggs
1 teasp cornflour
1 dessertspoon vanilla or sweet geranium sugar
½ pint creamy milk or half-cream

Put the milk in a pan and heat to just under boiling point. Beat the eggs, cornflour and sugar in a basin. Pour the hot milk on to the eggs, stirring continuously, then return all to the pan and set over the lowest heat. Stir constantly until the custard is thick enough to coat the back of a wooden spoon, but do not let it boil. If you want to keep it hot, put it in a basin over a pan of hot water. The small amount of cornflour minimises the risk of the custard curdling.

Wartime Christmas Pudding

6 oz breadcrumbs; 4 oz flour; 5 oz stoned and chopped prunes tossed in a little flour; 2 oz roughly chopped walnuts, or hazelnuts, or even beechnuts; 2 oz chopped orange rind; 4 oz suet; 3 oz coarsely chopped carrot; 4 oz honey, or syrup, or treacle; saltspoon salt; saltspoon baking powder; saltspoon nutmeg and the same of cinnamon; a little grated lemon rind. Mix all ingredients well with a little milk and steam for 4 hours. Allow to stand for a week and steam another 3 hours before serving. This is a very good recipe as it is not too sweet; I use toasted hazelnuts plus 2 oz chopped apple, and 3 tblsps brandy.

Gooseberry Fool

Set a Quart of Gooseberries on the Fire in about a Quart of Water. When they begin to simmer, and turn yellow, and begin to plump, throw them into a Cullender to drain the

Water out; then with the Back of a Spoon carefully squeeze the Pulp, throw the Sieve into a Dish, make them pretty sweet, and let them stand till they are cold; then take a Quart of new Milk, and the Yolks of two Eggs, with a little Nutmeg; stir it softly over a slow Fire till it simmers; take it off, and by Degrees stir it into the Gooseberries. Let it stand till it is cold. If you make it with Cream, you need not put Eggs in.

Richard Bradley, 1753

🍃 *Household Hints* 🍃

When making fruit pies place a straw through the hole in the centre to stop the juice boiling over.

Sprinkle a very little flour over the top of a cake to stop the icing running down the sides.

To keep mint fresh, hold it under a running tap for a few seconds, shake, then put it in a jamjar. Screw on the lid and turn the jar upside down to keep the air out.

Take extra care to protect sacks of root vegetables from the frost; pieces of old carpet or layers of newspaper, both under and over the sacks, will give extra protection in a garage or outhouse.

To cook potatoes and greens that have become frosted: prepare them as usual, but soak in cold water for an hour before cooking. Cook as usual, but with the addition of a small piece of saltpetre to the water. This worked well with frosted Brussels sprouts.

A wartime tip for making use of waste fat, cooked or raw: cover with cold water, bring it to the boil and boil hard until the water is reduced to less than a third. Put a sieve over a basin and pour the contents of the pan through. Leave to get cold, then the fat can be lifted off the top of the water beneath. The flavour can be improved by adding a sprig of rosemary to the fat as it is clarified.

To judge the (approximate) freshness of eggs: put an egg in a glass of water. If it is very fresh it will sink gently to the bottom; when about 3 weeks old it will lie on its side, the broad end slightly uppermost; when 3 months old it will stand upright in the water, the broad end showing just above the surface, and as it gets older still it will rise higher in the water (although by this time it may also have gone bad and will smell terrible even through the shell).

To keep butter cool, but not hard, in hot weather: stir ¼ oz saltpetre into 2 pints cold water and pour some into a soup plate. Stand the butter dish in the soup plate and invert a clean earthenware flower pot over it, and over the flower pot drape a clean handkerchief with the ends dipping in the saltpetre solution.

Rub freshly dug new potatoes in an old rough towel to remove the skins.

Rescue salty soup by bringing it slowly to the boil with slices of raw potato in it; when it boils, lift out the slices with a draining spoon and taste the soup. You can repeat this several times if necessary.

To keep your hands in good condition while preparing vegetables, and in particular new potatoes, rub them with lard or cooking oil before work, then wash them thoroughly with soap and water afterwards, or rub with a crust of bread soaked in vinegar (more hand-care tips on page 55).

Dry field mushrooms by threading the caps on strings and drying over the stove. Use the stalks for a mushroom ketchup (see page 87). Store carrots and beetroot unwashed in boxes of sand; cut the green fern from the carrots within about ½'' of the root, but twist off beetroot leaves (which make a good vegetable when fresh).

To prevent damaged beetroot from 'bleeding' while cooking, dip the cut or blemish in dry flour first.

Pulses (dried peas, beans, lentils, etc). Don't keep them too long—six months at the outside. Cook without salt, and add a pinch of bicarbonate of soda to help soften them and reduce the cooking time; add onions, carrots and herbs to flavour, then add salt only when they are done.

Winter Fuel

Gather sticks, twigs and tree prunings together. Break into pieces roughly equal in length, sawing the thicker bits, having regard to the size of your grate. Make these pieces of wood into bundles, with some dried leaves in the middle as stuffing, and binding the bundles along their length tightly with old string or binder twine. These bundles burn almost as long as logs, especially if used in conjunction with small coal or coal dust.

In winter, always set the handle of your pump as high as possible, before you go to bed. Except in very rigid weather, this keeps the handle from freezing. When there is reason to apprehend extreme cold, do not forget to throw a rug or horse-blanket over your pump; a frozen pump is a comfortless preparation for a winter's breakfast.

Mrs Child, 1833

Temporary repair for a dripping tap: half a large, raw potato, pushed firmly on the tap, so that it plugs it. Tie on tightly with tape or string. This lasted for over a fortnight in the hard winter of 1947.

A brick heated by the fire, then wrapped in an old sweater, makes a safe foot-warmer that doesn't turn cold and clammy in the night.

Very hard and durable candles are made in the following manner: melt together 10 oz of mutton tallow, a quarter of an ounce of camphor, 4 oz beeswax, 2 oz alum. Candles made of these materials burn with a very clear light.

Rushlights were made by peeling green rushes (leave on enough of the green outer skin to hold the pith together) and dipping them in any melted fat available. Mutton fat was considered the best as it dried hard and burnt with the clearest flame. The rush was dipped once or twice; if beeswax was obtainable, it was added to the mutton fat and improved the clarity of the flame, and the smell.

Night lights. To use a candle safely as a night light: light the wick, then sprinkle salt round the wick with a steady hand so that the flame is reduced to a safe glimmer. If the salt extinguishes the flame at this point it is very difficult to relight, but the method is effective and safe, since the salt will put out the flame immediately if the candle is knocked over.

To clean heavy woollen garments: buy about a pound of glue in slabs from a cabinet-maker; soak in cold water for twenty-four hours. Remove the glue from its soaking water and place in a vessel big enough to take the garments to be cleaned. Pour on to the glue a kettleful of boiling water and when the glue has melted, add cold water until the mixture is lukewarm. Place the garments, one at a time, in the vessel and move them about with a stick for about five minutes— do not press, rub or wring. The dirt will fall out. Lift out the garments and put through several rinses, all lukewarm, until the water is clear. Hang on hangers to drip dry, pulling the garments gently into shape as they dry, then little or no ironing will be necessary. Coats and skirts (tweed), silk dresses, woollen dresses and jumpers will turn out as fresh as if they had been to a cleaners. In fact, they turn out far better than if they had been to the cleaners; none of the natural qualities of the fibres are damaged and the dirt does indeed 'fall out'. This is a method my mother and grandmother used a good deal during the last war, and one which I would use far more if only cabinet-maker's glue in slabs was more easily obtainable.

Cushions for tired backs: collect the wool from fences and hedges of fields where sheep are kept, wash it to remove the lanolin, and when it is perfectly dry, use it to stuff small cushions. These are wonderfully firm and supportive, and warm—a nice present for anyone suffering from back trouble or rheumatism.

❧ *The Larder* ❧

In the country a good store-room is so indispensable that where there is none it ought to be built; it should be on the same floor with, and as near as possible to, the kitchen, and, as this would be on the ground floor, it would be necessary to make a cellar underneath, or to raise the building a little distance from the ground, to prevent its being damp, above all things to be guarded against, in a place where stores are kept. It may, perhaps, be kept dry by flues, from the kitchen fire; and this would be a saving of fuel and labour; but if not practicable, the room should have a fire place . . . For bottles of green gooseberries, peas, or any kind of fruit preserved dry, without sugar, have shelves with holes in them, to turn the bottles with their necks downwards. This effectually excludes the air.

Anne Cobbett, 1851

Bottling

Bottling still seems one of the best ways of preserving fruit, despite the advent of the freezer, since they will keep for at least four years. A jar of gooseberries in a fragrant elder-flower syrup is a delicious instant dessert, and rhubarb in ginger syrup topped with crumble is a warming winter pudding, assembled in seconds.

Basic method: wash and prepare the fruit; top and tail gooseberries (see page 51 for a quick method), cut rhubarb into 1″ lengths, strig currants, stone plums, damsons, cherries, apricots and peaches if liked, but it is not strictly necessary unless you are bottling fruit for shows. Pack the fruit into clean, wet, warm Kilner jars. Make up a syrup: about 8 oz sugar to 1 pint water, boiling hard for 5–10 minutes until it thickens. Add your chosen flavouring: elderflowers for gooseberries, ginger for rhubarb, cinnamon sticks for damsons and blackcurrants (or sweet geranium leaves for the latter), and any alcoholic flavouring, too. Sweet cider is nice with plums, brandy with peaches and apricots. Arrange the jars on a baking sheet lined with newspaper, so that they do not touch, then pour in boiling syrup to come within 1″ of the top of the jar. Put on the lids, but not the screw-bands, and put in the centre of the oven at 300°F. Cook for 1¼ hours, or until the fruit is soft. Take the jars out of the oven one at a time and stand them on a thick pad of newspaper, screwing on the screw-bands tightly. Leave to cool, then test for sealing by removing the bands and lifting the jar by the lid. If the lid is firmly attached to the jar, the seal is complete; wipe the jars, label clearly and store in a cool dry place. If the seal hasn't taken, either repeat the process with new lids—or store the contents in the freezer.

Fruit can be bottled without sugar, but the flavour is not as good; a wartime recipe for bottling syrup suggested two pounds of sugar to a gallon of water, with the addition of sweet cicely leaves for extra sweetness (strain the syrup before use).

To Preserve Strawberries in Wine

Put a quantity of the finest large strawberries into a goose-berry bottle, and strew in three large spoonfuls of fine sugar; fill up with Madeira wine, or fine sherry.

Mrs Rundell, 1818

Brandied Cherries

Choose ripe, sound cherries and leave a short length of stalk on each cherry 'to keep the juice in'. Put into wide-mouthed jars. Prepare a thick syrup with 1 lb sugar to 1 lb water and add 1½ pints of brandy to 1 pint of syrup. Pour over the cherries and cover the jars tightly, then leave for at least 6 months.

Damson Cheese

6 lbs damsons	2 cinnamon sticks
½ pint water	Sugar (see recipe)

Cook the damsons with the cinnamon sticks in the water until soft, over a low heat so that the fruit doesn't catch (or better still, bake them in the oven). Put through a food mill, removing the stones at the same time. Weigh the pulp and return it to the pan with 12 oz of sugar for each pound of pulp; heat gently to dissolve the sugar, then boil until the mixture begins to 'candy' round the edges, or until a wooden spoon drawn through the mixture leaves the bottom of the pan clean. Remove the pan from the heat and allow the purée to cool a little, then pour it into 8 oz plastic margarine tubs, filling each to within about ½ '' of the top and putting a disc of waxed paper over the surface before putting on the lids. Keep in a cool place for several months before eating; serve it with Stilton, or cream cheese, or stuck with blanched almonds and surrounded with thick cream. It is also good with cold duck or pork.

Medlar Cheese

2 lbs medlars
2 lemons
½ pint water

¾ lb sugar for each 1 lb pulp
Cinnamon stick
4 cloves

Wash the medlars and cut into quarters; grate the peel from the lemon and squeeze out its juice. Put the medlars, lemon peel and juice in a pan with the water and simmer until the fruit is soft. Put through a food mill and weigh the pulp, then proceed as in the recipe above, adding the spices with the sugar and removing them before potting.

Jams and Jellies

Mulberry and Apple Jam

2½ lbs apples
3 lbs mulberries

3 lbs sugar
1 pint water

Peel and core the apples and chop roughly. Put all the ingredients except the sugar in a preserving pan and cook to a pulp, then add the sugar and boil quickly for about 10 minutes until setting point is reached (a drop of the jam on a cold surface will wrinkle when pushed with a finger-tip). Pot in warm, dry jars.

Blackberry and Geranium Jelly

Blackberries
Water

Scented geranium leaves
Sugar

Cook the blackberries in enough water to cover them, until soft (for the best flavour cook slowly in a low oven, or in a crock-pot). Tip the contents of the pan into a jelly bag or an old clean pillowcase and hang up to drip into a bowl overnight. Next day measure the juice and put into a pan with 1 lb sugar to 1 pint juice, add 3 or 4 scented geranium leaves to each pint and bring slowly to the boil. Boil until setting point is reached—this jelly does not set very firmly. Keep tasting to see that the geranium flavour doesn't dominate that of the blackberries, and remove the leaves when the flavours balance. Pot as before.

Carrot Jam (also called Angel's Hair)

Carrots	Water
Sugar	Lemon juice and rind

Peel young carrots and cut into thick slices; cook until tender, strain and sieve or put through a food-mill. Weigh the pulp and to each pound add 1 lb sugar and the rind and juice of one lemon. Boil to setting point and pot.

Japonica Jelly

4 lbs japonica fruit	7 pints water
6 whole cloves	Sugar

Wash and slice the fruit and boil in the water with the cloves until soft. Tip into a jelly bag and leave to drip overnight. Next day, measure the juice into a preserving pan, add a pound of sugar to each pint, heat gently to dissolve the sugar then boil hard for ten minutes before testing for setting.

Rowan Jelly

Follow the recipe for japonica jelly, but add two or three apples for a firmer set if required, and keep the jelly for at least six months before using. It is delicious with mutton and lamb and all game.

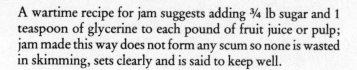

A wartime recipe for jam suggests adding ¾ lb sugar and 1 teaspoon of glycerine to each pound of fruit juice or pulp; jam made this way does not form any scum so none is wasted in skimming, sets clearly and is said to keep well.

Raspberry-Jamm

Take a pint of Currant Jelly, and a Quart of Raspberries, bruise them well together, set them over a slow Fire, keeping them stirring all the time till it boils; let it boil five or six Minutes, pour it into your Gallipots; paper as you do the Currant Jelly, and keep it for Use. They will keep so two or three Years and have the full Flavour of the Raspberry.

Richard Bradley, 1753

This is a very good jam indeed, and not too sweet. I can't vouch for the keeping qualities as ours is always eaten within the year.

Warmalade

Calculate 12 oz sugar and 1 pint water for each large Seville orange (about 3 oranges to the pound). Use a pressure cooker to cook the oranges whole, leave them to cool and then scoop out the pips. Slice the peel thinly and put in a large bowl with the cooking water and any remaining water from the amount given. Next day add the sugar and boil to a good set. This recipe was based on the wartime sugar allowance of 8 oz per person.

Lemon Curd

This recipe is suitable for retailing as it conforms to the standards set by the Preserves Order:

7½ oz unsalted butter
10 fl oz beaten egg (about 4 size 2 eggs)
10 fl oz lemon juice (about 7–8 lemons)
1 lb 9 oz sugar

Put the butter to melt in a large bowl over boiling water; when it has melted completely add the lemon juice and sugar, and stir until the sugar has dissolved. Remove from the heat and pour on to the lightly beaten eggs, stirring continuously. Strain the mixture back into the bowl over the pan of water and cook over a low heat until the mixture thickens. Pour into warm dry jars, fill to the brim, put a waxed disc on the top and cover completely when cold.

When preparing jams for showing, or selling, use preserving sugar for clarity, but for ordinary family use granulated sugar is cheaper. It is said that preserving sugar gives a jam better flavour as it dissolves more quickly and the jam consequently needs less cooking; I have not found this to be so to any noticeable degree, so perhaps modern sugar refining methods have narrowed the gap between the two products.

Pumpkin Cream

1 pumpkin	Grated rind and juice 1 lemon
Sugar	Grated rind and juice 2 oranges
Water	2 oz unsalted butter
1 teasp mace	½ teasp nutmeg
1 teasp ginger	

Peel the pumpkin, remove the seeds and cut into cubes. Simmer in a little water until tender. Drain well, then put through a food-mill. Weigh the pulp and add ¾ lb sugar to each pound of pulp, the grated orange and lemon rind and juice, the butter and spices. Boil until you have a thick cream—about 20 minutes. Pot in warm dry jars; use to fill flans and tarts. The same recipe can be used for marrow, but the flavour will not be as rich.

Candied Angelica

Use the young stems. Cut into 4'' lengths and simmer gently in a little water until tender. Remove the stalks from the pan but keep the cooking water. Strip off the outer skin and discard, return the angelica to the pan and simmer again until a bright green. Drain the stems well, then weigh them; taking 1 lb of caster sugar for every pound of angelica, arrange the stalks on a shallow dish and sprinkle the sugar over them. Leave for 2 days, then cook the stems and the sugar together for about 25 minutes. Remove the angelica, add another 2 oz sugar for each pound originally used, dissolve it in the syrup in the pan and boil it up for 5 minutes. Return the angelica to the syrup, simmer for 10 minutes, then arrange it on a cake rack to drain. Dry it off in a low oven (250°F), overnight, then store in waxed paper in an airtight jar.

Wartime Candied Peel

This must be used within a month, or it can be stored in the freezer well wrapped, and is much nicer than commercial peel.

Peel of 2 oranges and 2 lemons
8 oz sugar
Water

Peel the fruit thickly, but make sure there is no flesh left on it. Simmer the peel in plenty of water for about 1½–2 hours, or until tender; take a pint of the cooking water and dissolve the sugar in it to make a syrup. Add the peel and simmer it until the pith becomes clear—about 45 minutes to an hour. Drain the peel well and dry on a cake rack, in a low oven as for the angelica.

Pickles and Relishes

To pickle Mushrooms—Take the small Mushrooms, called Buttons, pare off the Dirt from the Stalks, wash them with water, and wipe them clean with a Flannel; then boil some Water and Salt; when it boils, put in the Mushrooms, and let them boil a Minute or two; then strain them through a Cullender; after which, make a Pickle of White-wine Vinegar, Mace, and Ginger; put them in, and stop them close up in Pots or Glasses, with a little Oil on them.

Richard Bradley, 1753

A good recipe which needs no twentieth-century alterations; the oil covers the top of the pickle and prevents it drying out.

Pickled Damsons

6 lbs damsons	1 oz cloves
4 lbs demerara sugar	1 oz cinnamon sticks
3 pints brown vinegar	

Prick the damsons all over with a fork and put them into a large bowl. Boil the vinegar, sugar and spices together for 10 minutes, pour over the damsons and leave for 24 hours. Pour off the vinegar into a pan, reboil and pour back over the damsons, leave another 24 hours. Repeat all this once more then pot and seal while hot. Keep 2–3 months before eating. Plums can be treated in the same way and both pickles are very good with cold ham and salt pork.

Pickled Brussels Sprouts

1 lb small tight very fresh sprouts
1 pint white malt vinegar
1 tblsp mixed pickling spices
1 oz sugar

Trim the sprouts, sprinkle with salt and leave overnight. Next day rinse them under a cold tap, drain well and pack them into clean dry jars. Bring the vinegar, spices and sugar to the boil, boil for 10 minutes and pour, hot, over the sprouts. Put a clean cloth over the jars, then remove and cover with airtight lids when cold; do not use metal lids for pickles as the vinegar rusts them. This is unusual and good; the quality of the sprouts is important, and they should be eaten within about 2 months.

To keep pickled onions white, add a few drops of almond oil to each jar.

To Pickle Herring or Mackerel
Cut off the Heads and Tails of your Fish, gut them, wash them and dry them well; then take two Ounces and a Half of Saltpetre, three quarters of an Ounce of Jamaica Pepper, and a quarter and half quarter of white pepper, and pound them small, an ounce of sweet Marjoram and Thyme chopp'd small; mix all together, and put some within and without the Fish; lay them in an earthen Pan, the Roes at Top and cover them with White-wine Vinegar, then set them into an Oven, not too hot, for two Hours.

The Lady's Companion

These will keep at least a fortnight in a fridge, about a week in a cool larder.

Pickling Seasons

Artichokes are in season in July & August
Cauliflowers in July & August
Capsicum pods, end of July & beginning of August
Cucumbers, the end of July to the end of August
French beans, July
Mushrooms, September
Nasturtium pods, middle of July
Onions from the middle to the end of July
Radish pods, July
Red cabbage, August
Samphire, August
Tomatoes, the end of July to the end of August.

Anne Cobbett, 1851

Pickled Walnuts

Walnuts are only fit for pickling as long as a darning needle can be pushed right through—traditionally, before 15 July. After this the shell begins to form and no amount of pickling will make them edible.

Let the green walnuts, pricked all over, soak in a strong brine (1 lb salt to 1 gallon water) for 4–5 days. Change the brine for a fresh lot and continue to soak for another 3 days.

Drain the walnuts and spread them on a flat dish, leave them until they turn black, turning them once or twice; this will take about 24 hours. Then pack into clean dry jars and cover with a cold spiced vinegar made as for the Pickled Sprouts, using brown vinegar and sugar rather than white.

NB. Wear rubber gloves while preparing the walnuts, as the stain is extremely stubborn and remains for weeks.

To pickle Nasturtium Seeds

Gather the Seeds when they are full grown and green, in a Dry Day, and lay them in Salt and Water for two or three

Days; then boil Vinegar, with some Mace, Ginger sliced, and a few Bay Leaves, for fifteen Minutes, and pour it boiling upon them covering them with a Cloth: and repeat the boiling of the Pickle, and scalding them with it for three Days successively: and when the last is poured on, let be cold before you cook it up.

Richard Bradley, 1753

These are very passable imitations of capers, and fun for children to do.

Mushroom Ketchup

3 lbs flat mushrooms	2'' cinnamon stick
3 oz salt	1 pint brown vinegar
2 teasps whole allspice	1 teasp black peppercorns
1 piece bruised ginger	4 blades mace
root	4 cloves

Sprinkle the mushrooms with the salt and leave overnight. Next day, rinse them briefly, drain well and chop finely. Put them in a pan with the remaining ingredients, put on the lid and simmer for half an hour. Strain and pour hot into warmed bottles (old ketchup bottles are ideal), cap tightly. Stand the bottles in a pan of simmering water for about 30 minutes to complete the sterilisation process, and for a really airtight seal, dip the bottle caps in melted wax. This is good added to soups, stews and sauces.

A Rich Chutney

2 lbs green gooseberries	8 oz figs
1 lb prunes	8 oz sultanas
8 oz onions	1 lb brown sugar
1 quart brown vinegar	2 oz ground ginger
1 level teasp cayenne	1 oz salt

Mince all the solid ingredients coarsely, add the sugar, ginger, cayenne, salt and vinegar. Bring all to the boil once the sugar has dissolved and cook until thick—about 45 minutes. Pot in warm dry jars and cover tightly.

Basil Wine

About the end of August fill a wide-mouthed bottle with fresh leaves of basil, cover with Sherry, and infuse them ten days; strain and put in fresh leaves, infuse another ten days, then pour off, and bottle it; A tablespoonful to a tureen of mock turtle, just before it is served.

Anne Cobbett, 1851

This is also very good added to casseroles of beef or game, and steak and kidney pie.

❧ *Winemaking* ❧

You will need somewhere warm to ferment the wine, then somewhere cool, but not cold, to store it. The equipment required is simple: gallon demijohns, plastic airlocks and the stoppers to hold them, a length of plastic tubing for siphoning, and plenty of empty bottles and good corks. A large jar of sodium metabisulphate is necessary for sterilising the bottles.

Wines

White Currant Champagne

1½ gallons water	4 lbs sugar
4 lbs white currants	½ oz yeast

Strig the currants. Boil the water and sugar together to make a syrup, add the currants, simmer for half an hour then leave to cool to lukewarm; add the yeast and leave to ferment for 48 hours. Strain into demijohns with airlocks and leave for about 6 months, then siphon off into clean bottles (follow the directions on the jar of sodium metabisulphate for sterilising and use with care—it is very unpleasant if inhaled), cork firmly and leave for another 6 months before drinking.

Fortified Cowslip Wine

Dried cowslip flowers can be obtained from good herbalists.

1 gallon cowslip flowers	Rind and juice 2 lemons
3 lbs sugar	Rind and juice 1 orange
1 gallon water	2 tblsps yeast
Brandy	

Boil the sugar and water for 10 minutes, add the cowslips, orange and lemon rind and juice. Cool to lukewarm, add the yeast and leave to ferment for 3–4 days. Strain, add ½ pint brandy to every gallon, keep for 2 months in a cask or demijohn, then bottle, and keep for about 3 months. As a tranquilliser, take 1 wineglassful mixed with 2 of hot water at bedtime.

Oak Leaf Wine

A curiosity, but said, by the donor of this recipe, to be excellent. Keep it to drink on Oak Leaf Day (29 May).

1 gallon oak leaves	2 gallons water
6 lbs sugar	2 sliced lemons
2 oz yeast	

Pick the oak leaves while they are still young, in about early June. Pour the boiling water over them and leave overnight.

Strain and add the sugar and lemons, boil for 30 minutes, remove the slices of lemon, cool to lukewarm and add the yeast. Leave for 12 days, then bottle in demijohns with airlocks and leave for 3 months. Bottle and keep a year.

Parsley Wine

Dry and light

1 lb freshly picked parsley	10 pints water
2½ lbs sugar	2 lemons
1 oz yeast	

Boil the parsley in the water for about 20 minutes. Strain into a plastic container and add the sugar and the sliced lemons, stirring until the sugar dissolves. Add the yeast when the liquid is lukewarm and leave to ferment, with a clean cloth over the container, for about 2 weeks, or until fermentation has ceased. Siphon into bottles, cork and keep a year.

Muscat Wine

Buy a medium dry white wine base from the chemist, and instead of using water as directed on the tin, make an infusion of elder flowers (6 fresh, fully opened heads to a gallon of water, simmered together for 25 minutes), cooled and strained, both for the initial addition and for topping up later on, following the instructions as directed on the label. You should end up with a white wine with a distinct flavour of muscat grapes from the elder flowers, for use as a dessert wine.

Gingerette

For this heartwarming recipe I am indebted to Sheila Hallas, who got it from her mother, Mrs Roddam, who in turn inherited it from her mother, Mrs Tabor: 'It leaves you speechless but warm in cold weather.'

2 quarts water	1 oz cinnamon stick
2 lbs demerara sugar	10 oranges
1 oz cloves	8 lemons
1½ oz chillies	Cochineal for colouring
1½ oz root ginger, bruised	

Dissolve the sugar in the water, and add the spices, tied in muslin. Simmer, after bringing to the boil, for 1½ hours. Add the juice of oranges and lemons, colour prettily with cochineal, strain, and bottle. Dilute to taste with hot water.

Marrow Rum

Leave a marrow on the plant until very large, the skin very hard, the flesh very ripe, and the whole very sound. Saw off about 2″ at the stalk end and keep this to use as a lid. Scoop out the seeds and replace them with demerara sugar. Stick the lid back on with sticking plaster, so that it is well sealed. Put the marrow in a large pillowcase and hang it up in a cool, dry place. After about a fortnight, take off the lid and fill up again with sugar—the first lot will have dissolved and eaten into the flesh of the marrow. Seal on the lid as before and hang up again. After another 6 weeks or so, the marrow will begin to drip as the sugar eats through the rind; enlarge the hole from which it is dripping and run the liquid into a clean demijohn with an airlock. Leave to ferment, then bottle and cork tightly. Keep for at least a year, then drink with care.

Sloe or Mulberry Gin

1 lb sloes or mulberries	1 cinnamon stick
1 lb caster sugar	Gin

Prick the sloes all over; mix the sloes or mulberries with the sugar, put into a jar with the cinnamon stick and top up with gin. Cap tightly and keep for 6 months, turning the jar from time to time. Strain into a bottle.

Richard Bradley's Cherry Brandy

In this Month (July) we have the Morello, and Black Cherry, ripe, which both are pleasant in Brandy, to those who would keep Drams by them: The way of making Black Cherry Brandy is only to pick the Cherries from the Stalks, and put them whole into the Brandy, about a Pound of Cherries to a Quart; this may remain for about a Month before it is fit to drink, and then the Brandy may be poured from the Cherries, and the Cherries put then into a Vessel of Ale, will make it extremely strong, only about the Proportion of a Pound of Cherries to a Gallon of Ale.

Richard Bradley, 1753

Cordials

Kentish Cordial

2 lbs damsons	2 pints water
1 lb elderberries	3 lbs sugar

Teaspoon cloves, a cinnamon stick, broken up, and a piece of nutmeg, all tied in a handkerchief.

Stone the damsons, pour the water over them and leave overnight. Next day, add the spices, bring to the boil, simmer for 25 minutes and pour over the elderberries. Leave overnight. Strain into a pan, add the sugar, heat slowly to dissolve, then bring to the boil and boil hard for 15 minutes. Cool and, when cold, bottle. To keep the cordial for a long time, stand the bottles, without touching, in a pan of boiling water for 25 minutes. When the bottles are completely cold, dip the tops in melted wax to make an airtight seal.

Plum Cordial

Equal amounts of plums and sugar
Almond essence
Brandy

Slit each plum with a sharp knife and put in a pan with the sugar. Heat gently until the sugar dissolves, then raise the heat and simmer until the plums are soft. Tip into a jelly bag or an old pillowcase and allow to drip, without pressing. Measure the syrup and for each pint add a small teaspoon of almond essence and two tablespoons of brandy. Bottle and use as a base for long drinks—top up with chilled white wine, or simply soda water.

Currant Cordial

8 oz blackcurrants   1 pint brandy
½'' dried ginger root   ½ lemon
3 oz caster sugar

Strig the currants into a jug, add the bruised ginger root and the rind of the half-lemon. Pour on the brandy and stir well, then cover the jug tightly and leave 48 hours. Strain and stir in the sugar until dissolved, then bottle. Keep 3–4 months before drinking. It is very good for colds and sore throats.

You can use the above recipe for making cordials from white and red currants, raspberries and wild strawberries. The drained fruit makes a very good ice-cream.

❧ The Stillroom ❧

The leisurely tasks of making pot pourri, toilet waters, sweet 'bagges', and other delights belong to another age, when the lady of the house often had a stillroom maid to help her, and a garden full of flowers and herbs grown expressly for the purpose. Nevertheless, it is fun to try, either growing the flowers and herbs yourself, or buying them ready dried from herbalists.

Distillates

For distillations, you will need simple equipment, much of which can be improvised: for example, a small camping gas stove standing on the draining board will support a small kettle which can be connected to a large glass jar (a demijohn is suitable) by means of rubber or plastic tubing and an airlock (remove the cover and connect the tubing to the funnel); this jar can be placed in the sink, under a gently running cold tap which will condense the steam from the kettle as it enters the jar. Place whatever herbs or flowers you like in the kettle, cover them with distilled water, connect the spout of the kettle to the jar with the tubing; set the kettle over a low flame and heat until the water in the kettle has steamed away, keeping the tap flowing over the sides of the jar. The liquid which forms in the jar will be your distillate.

Try distilling a mixture of rosemary, lavender and eau de cologne mint. Bottle the distillation and add it to a warm bath—it has a gentle and refreshing fragrance which is quite unlike the fierce synthetic scents of commercial bath additives.

Elder Flower Water
Cover fully opened flower heads with distilled water in the kettle and simmer over a low flame until all the water is used

94

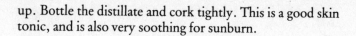

up. Bottle the distillate and cork tightly. This is a good skin tonic, and is also very soothing for sunburn.

Cucumber Skin Tonic

Peel and slice two large cucumbers and steam them until soft. Tie the cooked cucumber in a large clean cloth and squeeze all the juice into a measuring jug. Add a quarter of the amount of liquid of rectified spirits of wine (if you cannot obtain this, use whisky instead, I was told), and one third of elder flower water. Bottle and shake well before use; use frequently at first, then regularly once a day. For dry skins, omit the spirits of wine (or whisky).

Herbal Bath Vinegar

This is very refreshing in hot weather.

> ¼ pint cider vinegar
> ¼ pint water
> Sprigs fresh rosemary, thyme, lavender and bergamot

Put all the ingredients into a pan and infuse over a low heat for about 15 minutes, then remove from the heat and leave to cool. Or, alternatively, put all the ingredients into the distilling kettle and heat until the liquid in the kettle has evaporated. In either case, use it to scent a bath, or as a final rinse for dark hair.

To Make Essential Oils

Saturate the distillate with ordinary coarse salt; the oil will float to the top and can be skimmed off. This method only yields tiny amounts; the following ones produce more generous quantities, although they are not quite as strong.

Soak cotton wool in an odourless oil such as almond. Arrange a layer of the cotton wool in a screw-top jar, then cover it with a thick layer of the petals of the flowers whose scent you require. Continue to layer the oil-soaked cotton wool and flowers until the jar is full, then screw on the cap and leave it in the sun for a week or more. Throw away the flowers and squeeze the oil into a small jar to use as required for pot pourri, bath oils and so on. Press the cotton wool between blotting paper to remove all traces of oil, then use to scent drawers and cupboards.

Put the flower petals in a small jar of almond oil and leave in the sun for a week, strain and use.

Take the flowers of Spike and wash them only in oyl olive, and then stamp them well, then put them in a canvas bag, and press them in a press as hard as you can and take that which cometh out carefully, and put it into a strong vessel of glass, and set it in the Sun, for it will clear of it self, and wax fair and bright, and will have a very sharp odor of the Spike; and thus you may make oyl of other herbs of like nature, as Lavender, Camomile, and such like.

Gervase Markham, 1653

'Spike' is spikenard or centaury, which has a fresh, bitter and very aromatic smell.

Pot Pourri

Basic Pot Pourri
Collect the petals of old fashioned roses (page 27), some lavender flowers, carnation petals, some sprays of myrtle, thyme and sweetbriar, a few scented geranium leaves, two or three sprigs of rosemary and lemon balm and eau de cologne

96

mint. Spread these between sheets of newspaper to dry in the sun, or in an airing cupboard. Grate the rind of 2 lemons and 2 oranges and dry in the same way. When all the above ingredients are quite dry, mix with about 1 lb coarse salt, ½ lb sea-salt, 1 oz powdered orris root, ½ teaspoon each of ground allspice (*not* mixed spice) and ground cloves, ¼ teaspoon nutmeg. Put in a large pot pourri jar and leave, with the lid on, for about a week, stirring once or twice. When the pot pourri is ready, keep it in its lidded jar, removing the lid only when you want it to scent the room; if you leave the jar uncovered the scent will soon go.

Pot pourri can be revived by adding a few drops of a reviver oil of whatever scent you like: rose, lavender, bergamot, jasmine, or blends, which can either be bought or made at home.

To add colour and texture to pot pourri, add the dried heads of small everlasting flowers such as helichrysum or statice, dried rose-buds, marigold, bergamot and nasturtium petals, daisy heads and pinks. To dry flower heads to preserve colour: line two 12″ squares of small mesh wire netting with wadding, tacking it firmly through the wire. Sandwich the flower heads between the wadding and tie the netting together to make a lightweight flower press, then hang in the sun, or an airing cupboard.

Sachets and Pillows

A Bag to Smell unto for Melancholy, or to cause one to sleep. Take dried Rose leaves, keep them close in a glasse which will keep them sweet, then take powder of Mints, powder of

Cloves in a grosse powder, and put the same to the Rose leaves, then put all these together wi'n a bag, and take that to bed with you and it will cause you to sleep, and it is good to smell unto at other times.

W. Ram, 1606

Fragrant Sleep Sachets

Make this mixture into a small sachet flat enough to slip between pillow and case. Put into an electric blender 2 cups dried pine needles, 1 cup dried rosemary and 1 cup lemon balm, and blend until finely powdered.

Dried lavender and mint, in equal quantities, make a good alternative. For anyone who suffers from insomnia, make sachets of dried hops; although the smell of hops is not attractive to everyone, their effect is undoubtedly soporific.

Herbal Bath Sachets

These make good presents, particularly to those who live in hard water areas as the oatmeal they contain softens the water. Mix 1 oz powdered orris root with 2 oz dried lavender and 3 oz medium oatmeal and sew firmly into small bags of fine muslin. Add one to the bath as the taps are running. Variations: your favourite pot pourri mixture added to twice as much oatmeal; dried sweet briar and scented geranium leaves; mint, southernwood and rosemary.

For linen cupboard sachets, lavender alone is still one of the nicest and easiest to make, but the following blend is something a little more special; it also makes a good sachet to put amongst men's clothes as it is rather more masculine than many of the sweet mixtures.

Mix ½ lb dried lavender, 1 oz dried lemon thyme, 1 oz dried mint, ½ oz dried cloves, 1 oz dried bay-leaves and 1 oz cooking salt and fill small bags or sachets.

Sweet Herb Bags

Take equal amounts of the following dried herbs—scented geranium (rose or lemon), lemon balm, rosemary, bergamot, thyme, mint, bay, lavender and sweet briar—and mix with quarter quantities of salt, ground cloves, cinnamon and grated dried orange peel.

To make a Sweet-Bag for Linen

Take of Orris roses, sweet Calamus, cypress roots, of dried Lemon-peel, and dried Orange-peel; of each a pound, a peck of dried roses; make all these unto a gross powder, coriander-seed four ounces, nutmegs an ounce and a half, an ounce of cloves; make all these into fine powder and mix with the other; add musk and ambergris; then take four large handfuls of lavender flowers dried and rubbed; of sweet-marjoram, orange-leaves, and young walnut-leaves, of each a handful, all dried and rubb'd; mix all together, with some bits of cotton perfum'd with essences, and put it up into silk bags to lay with your Linnen.

The Compleat Housewife

That is a very sophisticated recipe, and an approximation of it makes a very good stuffing for a bedroom cushion. To make these you will need, apart from a pot pourri mixture, lengths of the terylene wadding used for quilting, and pretty cotton fabric for the cover. Fold a length of wadding into three to make an envelope, tacking the sides firmly and, after adding the herb mixture, tacking down the flap firmly to enclose the mixture. Make your cotton case to fit this pad, making it as decorative as you like as long as it is washable. To wash the cushion, empty the wadding carefully into a large plastic carrier bag and fasten the neck. If the filling has lost its scent, renew it at the same time (the fragrance will last about nine months to a year, gradually lessening as the weeks pass).

🌿 *The Medicine Chest* 🌿

A list of herbs for medicinal use; * indicates a plant attractive enough to add to an herbaceous border.

*Angelica: a good cough and cold remedy, and will treat wind and colic either as a syrup or as a tea.

*Arnica (or Leopard's Bane): for outward use only, but an excellent lotion for sprains, bruises and chilblains provided the skin is unbroken. It is a powerful irritant to which some people are allergic. It has very attractive bright yellow flowers in late spring.

*Balm: promotes curative sweating in colds and 'flu, and as a tonic herb is often included, like borage, in wine cups.

*Caraway: the seeds pounded and warmed make an effective poultice for ear and toothache, and bruises. They are also good digestives.

Comfrey: also known as 'boneset' or 'knitbone' because of its old use as a poultice to heal broken limbs. Wrap a few bruised comfrey leaves round a fresh sprain and see how effective it is. It is also held to be a cure for arthritis.

*Elecampane: 'is good for shortnesse of breathe and an old cough, and for such as cannot breathe unless they hold their neckes upright.—The root preserved is good and wholesome to the stomack; being taken after supper it doth not onely helpe digestion, but also keepeth the belly soluble.' John Gerard, 1633
It is a very handsome, tall plant for the back of a border.

*Fennel: another of the umbelliferous group of herbs which help the digestion. A syrup of the seeds was used for coughs, and the powdered seeds were used against fleas in stables.

Garlic: Culpeper says, 'A remedy for all diseases and hurts.' Singers swear by garlic syrup as a cure for hoarseness: infuse ½ lb sliced garlic in 1 pint water overnight; next day, strain and add ½ lb sugar, then simmer to a syrup. Chew fresh parsley afterwards to sweeten the breath.

*Hyssop: apply the fresh leaves, bruised, to help heal cuts. The tea braces a weak stomach.

*Marsh-mallow: use the tea for urinary infections such as cystitis, and the leaves also for bruises and sprains. It is an ingredient of skin tonics, used for its softening effect.

*Rue: the juice of the bruised leaves was used to calm 'nervous fancies', and a leaf or two, chewed, soothes a nervous headache. It will also ease sciatica. It makes an attractive plant if kept tidy by trimming off the yellow flower heads, but its smell is pungent and is either loved or loathed.

*Southernwood: has a very aromatic smell which is said to dispel drowsiness, which explains its inclusion in posies carried to church by Victorian ladies. It is also good for curing worms in children and, 'boiled in barley meal it taketh away pimples'. Culpeper

Wormwood: very bitter, but an excellent tonic for poor digestion (it is a main ingredient of vermouth); the tea is recommended for jaundice. The leaves have antiseptic properties.

The Infusions or Spirits drawn from dried Herbs are more free from the Earthly and Watery Parts than the Infusions or Spirits drawn from green Herbs. I observe that in making such Infusions as Teas of dried Herbs, the best way is to pour boiling Water upon them, and in half a Minute at most, pour out the Water again from the Herbs, such Tea will then be of a fine green Colour, and full of Spirit; but if the Herbs stand longer with Water upon them the Water will change of a brownish Colour, will lose the fine flavour of the Herb, and become ill-tasted.

Richard Bradley, 1753

Treatments and Cures

A Refreshing Drink in a Fever
Put a little tea-sage, two sprigs of balm, and a little wood-sorrel, into a stone jug, having first washed and dried them: peel thin a small lemon and clear from the white; slice it, and put a bit of the peel in; then pour in three pints of boiling water, sweeten, and cover it close.

Mrs Rundell, 1818

For a Sad Heart
Pick the petals of red roses, violets, borage and anchusa, and dry. Store in an air and light-tight container. When feeling depressed, put 3 tablespoons in a teapot, cover with boiling water and infuse under a teacosy for 1 minute. Sweeten with honey if necessary and drink to your heart's content.

Hop Tea
For a poor appetite and strained nerves. Pour a pint of boiling water over 1 oz dried hops, add half a lemon, sliced, and a dessertspoon of glucose. Leave to cool. Take a wineglassful half an hour before meals. For insomnia drink the same amount, hot, in bed.

Leek Milk

Use the green tops. Slice and wash thoroughly, cover with milk and simmer until tender. Season lightly and drink hot for a cold.

For the Dry Cough

Take of clean wheat and of clean Barley of each a like quantity, and put them into a gallon and a half of fair water, and boyl them till they burst, then strain it into a clean vessell, and add thereto a quarter of fine Lycoras powder and two pennyworth of gumme Arabick, then boil it over againe and straine it, and keep it in a sweet vessel, and drink thereof morning and evening.

Gervase Markham, 1653

For Whooping Cough

Dissolve a whole egg, shell and all, in lemon juice. It will take about 2 lemons and 36 hours. Strain and add 2 dessert-spoonfuls of honey and the same amount of glycerine. Take a teaspoon at a time to help relieve the cough.

Remedy for Consumption

Take 20 Snails, and a Handful of broad Daisies, put in a Quart of Water, and gently boil it to a Pint; take a Spoonful every Morning in some Milk.

Richard Bradley, 1753

For Diarrhoea and Fever

Mix the whites of 2 eggs well with 1½ pints of cold water, sweeten to taste and add a little brandy if advisable.

Pick-me-up
Beat an egg white stiff, add 2 teaspoons of brandy, 4 of cream and a pinch of caster sugar.

For Chilblains
Drink burgundy twice a day as soon as they appear, and cut an onion in half, dip it in salt and rub the chilblain with this. 'Do not wash off until obliged.'

For any Venome in the Ear
Take the juyce of lovage, and drop it into the ear, and it will cure any venome, or kill any worme, earwig or other vermine.

Gervase Markham, 1675

To Prevent a Cold
Mix as much cinnamon as will stay heaped on a sixpence (a new penny, now) with hot lemon juice (add 2 soluble aspirins to this last thing at night).

For a Liverish Headache
1 teaspoon Worcester sauce in a tumbler of soda water, to be drunk while it effervesces.

The Toothache
Take two or three Dock roots, and as many Daisie roots, and boil them in water till they be soft, then take them out of the water, and boyl them well over again in Oyl Olive, then strain them through a clean cloth, and anoint the pained tooth therewith, and keep your mouth close, and it will not onely take away the Pain, but also ease any megrim or grief in the head.

Gervase Markham, 1675

Puffballs sliced and applied as a poultice draw pus from wounds to promote clean healing. They were also applied to chilblains.

Coltsfoot is well known as a cough reliever, but the smoke from the burning leaves was said to relieve pain too. It is often included in home-made pipe tobacco.

Pennywort was used by country children to soothe grazes.

Turnip was often used as a substitute for glycerine, when none was available, in treating chest complaints. A few slices, put in a bowl and covered with sugar, yielded a liquid which was bottled and kept.

A poultice of burdock leaves boiled in vinegar is soothing for tired and sore feet.

For lumbago, take 2 drops oil of juniper on a spoonful of sugar first thing in the morning.

The rough side of a cabbage leaf will draw a wound, the smooth side will heal it.

A poultice made of sanicle leaves, dry or fresh, 'heals green wounds'. It is regarded as a sort of universal panacea, and should be grown in every garden.

The Farmyard and Smallholding

The life of the farm was held together and directed quite as much by the farmer's wife as by the farmer himself, a fact which Thomas Tusser recognised, frequently addressing himself to her in his *Five Hundred Points of Good Husbandry*. Dairy work, poultry and bee-keeping, bacon curing and cheese-making, as well as the care of a large household of farm hands in addition to her own family, all came under her aegis.

Until the First World War, farms were almost entirely self supporting and no farmer's wife would have needed her card to the hypermarket, as she does now. Last year, in France, we saw a farm of this old school. It was of the so-called 'inefficient' sort that our farmers hate to subsidise—the yard held pigs, chickens, geese, ducks, turkeys, goats and one or two sheep. Ranged against the wall of the enormous barn were tier upon tier of rabbit hutches (to the delight of my daughter, until she understood the unsentimental view the French have of the rabbit solely as an ingredient of pâtés and terrines). Father and son farmed the land with the help of an antique tractor—the horse had died the year before, leaving an unfillable gap—while grandmother, mother and daughter reared the calves, piglets and lambs, kept the poultry and rabbits, milked the cows and goats, turned the home-produced pork into *rillettes* and *confits*, made their own bread, butter and cheese. The milk was sold, unpasteurised, to neighbours such as our friends, who bicycled up for it every other day with litre-sized milk churns swinging from the handlebars. In the autumn the Boisgard family supple-mented their already varied diet with chestnuts and fungi collected in the enormous forests bordering their land. It was a shock to return to England and our neighbouring farm, which I examined with new eyes. On an acreage twice the size of M Boisgard's, a herd of cows (units) grazed on a substance that looked more like green raffia than grass, produced with the help of lavish doses of nitrogen. A few potatoes were grown, a few turkeys raised for Christmas—all very efficient according to the rules of the EEC, but amazingly unproductive compared to the cornucopia of the Boisgards' farm.

I make no apologies for including old farming advice in this chapter: modern farming is a soulless business, as anyone who listens to BBC Radio 4's farming programmes early in the morning will know. Even the Archers refer to their cows by numbers—'32 is off her feed this morning'—and I'm sure few farmers think about the pleasure their 'cared-for' hens would get from wandering about in the sunshine (see page 114 for Henry Stephens' piece of advice on that score). We are constantly told that the romantic view of farming does not provide enough for the world's needs, but judging by

107

the landscape of lakes and mountains of surplus food that is produced by 'efficient' farming, perhaps a happier medium is required.

🌿 *The Dairy* 🌿

Of all the appendages to a country dwelling, there is nothing which so successfully rivals the flower garden, in exciting admiration, as a nice dairy. From the show-dairy, with its painted glass windows, marble fountains and china bowls, to that of the common farm house, with its red brick floor, deal shelves, and brown milk pans, the dairy is always an object of interest, and is associated with every idea of real comfort, as well as of imaginary enjoyment, attendant upon a country life.

Anne Cobbett, 1851

Elder bushes were left to grow under the windows of a dairy, as the flowers were thought to keep flies from entering, and in any case, elder was powerful magic against witches.

A cow of the smallest sort common in England will not require above 70 or 80 lbs of good moist food in the twenty-four hours [this was often partly composed of cabbages, specially grown, as well as pasture]. And what a produce is that of a cow! I suppose only an average of 5 quarts of milk a day. If made into butter, it will be equal every week to two days of the man's wages, besides the value of skim milk.

William Cobbett

Cobbett may have been referring to the Dexter cow, a small 'cottage-sized' breed, now enjoying a revival with the boom in self-sufficiency.

Green parsnip tops fed to the cows produce good creamy milk, as do the cabbages referred to above; care must be taken to remove any rotten leaves as they will taint the milk.

Milk

The first milk from a cow after her calf is born is called 'beestings'; it is particularly rich and considered a delicacy and many are the recipes for beestings tarts and custards. 'It makes the best Yorkshire pudding,' one friend told me, and another that, with sugar added and slowly baked in the oven, beestings (or 'beastings', as it is spelt in some parts of the country) pudding was something worth waiting for. A jugful was often given as a present to a close friend, or to an invalid, with the injunction that the jug be returned un-washed. To wash the jug might bring about the death of the new-born calf.

A cow should be milked clean. Not a drop, if it can be avoided, should be left in the udder. It has been proved that the half pint that comes out last has twelve times as much butter in it as the half pint that comes out first.

William Cobbett

A friend who remembers life as a Land Girl in Shropshire during the last war also remembers the abundance of milk—two pints a day formed part of the farm worker's wages, as well as a row of potatoes in the field and 'a glass of whisky on Christmas morning, after milking'.

A Curd Star

Set a quart of new milk upon the fire with two or three blades of mace; and when ready to boil, put it to the yolks and whites of nine eggs well beaten, and as much salt as will lie upon a small knife's point. Let it boil till the whey is clear; then drain it in a thin cloth, or hair sieve; season it with sugar, and a little cinnamon, rose-water, orange-flower water, or white wine, to your taste; and put into a star form, or any other. Let it stand some hours before you turn it into a dish; then put round it thick cream or custard.

Mrs Rundell, 1818

Junket

1 pint milk fresh from the cow
1 teasp rennet
1 tblsp sugar

Heat the milk to blood heat, then remove from the heat and stir in the rennet and sugar until the sugar dissolves. Leave in a warm place to set—about 2–3 hours. A recipe from Devon suggests the addition of a spoonful of rum or brandy before serving the junket with clotted cream.

Cream

Clotted cream is made by heating the rich Devon milk very gently, in wide shallow dishes, and skimming the cream off the top. A separator is not used.

Thunder and lightning: clotted cream and golden syrup piled on to buttered 'splits' or 'chudleighs'—Cornish and Devon tea-cakes.

110

Butter

Gentle, constant churning gave the creamiest butter; violent motion made it greasy. The churn would be warmed with hot water in the winter, and cooled with cold in the summer, before butter making.

For my own use, I would never desire better butter, all the year round, than that churned every morning in a small churn from sweet cream. Such butter, on cool new-baked oatcake, overlaid with flower virgin honey, accompanied with a cup of hot, strong coffee mollified with crystallised sugar and cream, such as the butter has been made from, is a breakfast worth partaking of.

Henry Stephens, 1855

Whey is excellent food and drink for pigs in summer, and particularly for a brood-sow, when suckling pigs. It forms a safe aperient for dogs—no better medicine can be given daily to a pack of fox-hounds out of the hunting season.
Transactions of the Highland and Agricultural Society, 1847

Cheese

Dock leaves were used to wrap dairy produce for market.

Dairy floors were scrubbed with green nettle tops as it was thought this would produce the blue cheese moulds required for Stilton, Blue Cheshire, Blue Vinny, and similar cheeses.

111

The roots of alkanet, *pentaglottis sempervirens*, were used to colour the 'red' cheeses, such as Red Leicester, and this plant can often be found growing still in the gardens of old farm houses. It has small bright blue flowers, white centred, and very prickly hairy green leaves.

August—Examine your Cheese-loft, and turn your Cheeses, rubbing them well with a dry cloth; and if you find them infested with Mites, cut them out, and fill up the Holes with fine Powder of Chalk, taking care that you leave none of the Mites upon the Shelves. This should be done once or twice in every hot Month.

Richard Bradley, 1753

Making hard cheese is a lengthy process, but certainly one worth trying if you have access to large amounts of milk. A good book on the subject is Batsford's *Making Cheeses* by Susan Ogilvy.

To make Cottage Cheese
Untreated milk can be left to go sour by itself, and pasteurised milk can be 'turned' by the addition of 1 teaspoon of rennet to 1 pint warmed milk. When the milk is thick, add salt to your taste and turn it into a *boiled* cloth; hang this up and leave the cheese to drip into a bowl overnight. Next day, scrape the cheese off the cloth and add chopped fresh herbs if you like, or leave the cheese plain and form it into a neat pat. It is traditional to serve it on green hazel or beech leaves.

Nettle cheese was matured between layers of fresh nettles, the nettles being changed every two days. The cheese thus

112

matured should be a small one, 'not above half an inch' in depth and can be made according to the cottage cheese method. 'The finest summer cheese which can be eaten.'

Gather your nettles as much without stalkes as may be, for the more even and fewer wrinkles that your cheese hath, the more dainty is your Housewife accounted.

Gervase Markham, 1653

❧ *The Poultry Yard* ❧

Hens

As a rough guide to the number of hens to keep, have twice as many hens as members of the household—any surplus eggs in the spring and summer can usually be sold without much trouble.

The hen-wife should visit every nest, and collect the eggs every day; and the time for collecting the largest number of eggs and disturbing the poultry the least, is in the afternoon between 2 and 3 o'clock, before the birds begin to retire to roost. A nest-egg should be left in every nest, as it is an established fact, that hens prefer to lay in nests containing eggs to those which are empty—Eggs are most conveniently collected in small hand-baskets, and a short light ladder will afford easy access to nests situated above reach from the ground. Nine eggs weigh about a pound.

Henry Stephens, 1855

Nine size 3 eggs still weigh about a pound; size 2 eggs weigh about 2–2¼ ozs each (see the 'Rule-of-Egg Cake' on page 66).

Dealing with a broody hen: make a nest with a firm framework of wire-netting against rats, and a lining of bracken (not hay, as, according to Richard Bradley, 'hay is apt to make the sitting Hens faint and weak'), and sacking to keep out any draughts. Dust the nest with pepper to keep vermin away, and don't forget to add a few sprigs of rue, to guard against witches. Sprinkle the selected eggs with a little warm water to make the shells easier for the emerging chicks to chip through, then settle the hen on top of the eggs.

In Cornwall, a chain round the barn or hen-house, about six inches from the ground, was believed to be good protection against rats; whether the height of the chain was a deterrent, or whether it was magic connected with the iron of the chain, isn't clear.

Richard Bradley has a curious way of persuading capons to rear a brood of chicks: 'It is done by plucking the Feathers off his Breast and rubbing the bare skin with Nettles, and then putting the Chickens to him, which will presently run under his Breast, either allay the Stinging and Itching or contribute at least to warm that Part from which the feathers were pulled. A Capon, once accustomed to this Service, will not easily leave it off; but as soon as he has brought up one Brood of Chickens, we may put another to him; and, when they are fit to shift for themselves, we may give him the Care of a third.'

As soon as the grass begins to grow in spring, so early will cared-for hens delight to wander into sheltered positions of pasture, in the sunshine, in the warm side of a thorn-hedge, and pick the tender blades, and devour the worms, which the genial air may have warmed into life and activity. With such morsels of spring food, and in pleasant temperature, their combs will begin to redden, and their feathers assume a glossy hue; and even by February they will begin to chant— and this is a sure harbinger of the commencement of the laying season.

Henry Stephens, 1855

Waterglass remains one of the best ways of preserving eggs and is still available from good old-fashioned ironmongers and chemists. Make up the solution according to the instructions and pour it into a stoneware crock or a plastic bucket. Wipe (don't wash) the eggs clean—they should be between 1 and 3 days old—and immerse them in the waterglass. They will keep for about 9 months, and are best used for cakes etc, rather than eaten boiled or fried.

A chicken never eats more tenderly than when killed a short time before being dressed.

Henry Stephens, 1855

But an old fowl should hang a week before cooking, and if a hen cannot be eaten quickly after killing, it should be hung for up to four days (in winter).

The easiest method of catching a hen is at night, when it is roosting, using a torch as the bright light will stupefy it.

One may now (April) produce a Cross-strain of Fowls, between a Cock Pheasant and the Hens of common Poultry,

115

if we keep a Cock Pheasant in Company with six or seven Hens, in a place where there can be no other Mixture: the Fowls bred from these will be of a delicate Flesh.

Richard Bradley, 1753

Ducks

I buy a troop when they are young, and put them in a pen, and feed them upon oats, cabbages, lettuces, and water, and have the place kept very clean.

William Cobbett

This last point is important as ducks are dirty feeders. Use duck eggs only in dishes which need long cooking, such as fruit cakes.

Sexing ducks is difficult, but—the females quack, the males either hiss or 'creak'.

Geese

Geese were often kept as watchdogs as they will always make a considerable racket at the approach of strangers, and are very intimidating.

A goose at Michaelmas was regarded as a natural perquisite by farm labourers. Geese were turned out on to the stubble after harvest to fatten on the gleanings; up until this time a goose was termed 'green', as it would be feeding on grass. Hens, too, would be 'stubbled'; they would be put out, coop and all, to pick up the fallen corn.

Goose is experiencing something of a revival, at Christmas if not at Michaelmas. 'They can be kept to advantage only where there are green commons, and there they are easily kept; live to a very great age, and are amongst the hardiest animals in the world.'

William Cobbett

Turkeys

Turkeys are a good deal less hardy than geese, and young turkeys in particular must be protected from cold and damp. They are hatched in May and fattened for consumption at Christmas. 'The varieties in common use are white, black, or mottled grey: and of these the white yields the fairest and most tender flesh.'

Henry Stephens, 1855

Pigeons

Pigeons were kept by most large households as 'convenience' food—they were ready to eat all the year round and, being small, could be cooked quickly for unexpected guests, although plucking a pigeon is not a particularly fast business.

Poultry Feathers

The feathers of most farmyard fowl were carefully kept, to fill mattresses, pillows and coverlets; goose down was the most highly prized, followed by duck down. The washed feathers were frequently put to dry in the bread oven after the bread had finished baking.

There is no need to send duvets and pillows to the cleaners if you have the space to wash them at home. A lukewarm solution of *soapy* water (not detergent) is needed, and it is best to wash the largest articles in the bath. Hang the articles on the line to dry in the fresh air, fluffing them up, and shaking them as they dry. A friend dries her down-filled anorak in the tumble-dryer with a tennis ball for company (on the lowest heat setting) as she says it helps to distribute the feathers evenly.

Old pillows can be revived by emptying the feathers into an old pillowcase, washing the pillow-tick and when it is dry, rubbing a bar of yellow soap, or a candle, all over the wrong side, paying particular attention to the seams, to make the ticking feather-proof again. Wash the feathers in an old pillowcase, then remove them and spread them out on sheets of newspaper to dry—an attic is the best place as it is dry and there is least risk of draught there. When they are perfectly dry, stuff them back into the clean and reproofed ticks. It is advisable to keep the feathers of separate articles apart, so that the same amount of feathers will be returned. My mother remembers the nuns at her convent school revived the feather mattresses and pillows in this way, each year.

❧ *Bee-Keeping* ❧

Keeping bees is not to be entered into without careful thought and reading. HMSO publish several good booklets: *Bee-keeping*, *Beehives*, *Honey from Hive to Market*, *Diseases of Bees*, which are available from HMSO bookshops. Contact your local College of Agriculture, who may be able to put you in touch with their Bee-Keeping Instructor, or with bee-keepers in the area.

Thomas Tusser's advice on placing the hives is still relevant:

Set hive on a plank, not too low by the ground
Where herb with the flowers may compass it round;
And boards to defend it from north and north east
From showers and rubbish, from vermin and beast

Position the hives in a quiet, sunny place away from animals, and from passers-by who may come into contact with the homing bees.

In bad winters, and summers too, feed the bees with a syrup of 1 lb sugar in 1 pint water, and when removing the honey, leave enough in the hive for the bees. Provide water as well, somewhere near the hive.

At this Season (November) you must take care to keep your Bees warm, and feed your weak Stocks; you may thatch the Common Hives with Straw, and you may put some dry Straw between.

Richard Bradley, 1753

Bees never thrive in a quarrelsome family.

For honey in the first year, buy a large swarm (about 7 lbs weight) as early as possible in May (remember—'A swarm of bees in May, Is worth a load of hay'). For honey in the second year, you can start with a small swarm later in the summer and build up the swarm and your confidence at the same time.

Only gold coins should be used when buying bees; failing that, payment should be in kind.

The flavour and colour of the honey depends on the flowers supplying the nectar: heather honey is dark and strong, clover paler and more delicate; lime-flowers produce particularly good honey. All the nectar-supplying flowers should be as near the hive as possible so that the bees do not have to expend too much energy in seeking it. Lemon balm (also called bee-balm) is much loved by bees, as is hyssop and rosemary—plant as much as you can around the hives.

Products

'Comb' honey fetches the highest price; 'chunk' honey, where a piece of the comb is included in a jar of liquid honey, is also popular. Extractors are expensive to buy, but can often be borrowed. Or buy one to share among a group of fellow bee-keepers.

The old method of extracting honey was to break sections of the comb into a linen bag, hang this up and leave it to drip into a bowl. This was the 'virgin' honey. The remaining honeycomb was broken smaller and hung near a source of heat so that it dripped more freely; it was then, finally, squeezed to produce the last drops.

Honey is excellent in cakes as it keeps them moist. It produces a well-flavoured jam, although one that sets less well, and may burn more easily, than jam made with sugar. You can compromise by using $^2/_3$ sugar to $^1/_3$ honey.

Mead

1 lb honey	1 oz yeast
8 oz dried hops	1 gallon water

Dissolve the honey in the warmed water, add the hops and simmer for about 35 minutes. Cool to lukewarm and add the yeast. Cover and leave for 3–4 days before straining into a jar with a fermentation lock. When fermentation ceases, bottle and keep for a year.

Equal parts of turps and honey, dotted about lofts and attics in jar-lids, is said to expel bats.

Separate beeswax by heating the empty comb in water until the wax melts and floats to the surface. Cool and lift off the wax when it has set.

Fill holes in wood with beeswax—melt equal quantities of wax and rosin (very carefully, as it is inflammable), and cool until you have a workable substance. Use this to fill the hole, allow to harden, then finish with fine emery paper.

Farmers' Dubbin

Melt a lump of mutton fat with twice as much beeswax, and when the mixture is cool but still liquid, paint it on to boots, working it well into the seams and the join between sole and upper.

A soothing treatment for arthritic fingers is to dip them in a bowl of warm beeswax, melted over a pan of hot water. It is also an old remedy for gout, painted, while still warm, on to the affected area.

A very old form of waterproof wrapping was made from linen soaked in melted beeswax—the modern counterpart is the waxed cotton used for waterproof clothing.

Eggs were coated in beeswax to preserve them.

☙ *Pig-Keeping* ☙

. . . but bacon is the great thing. It is always ready; as good cold as hot; goes to the field or the coppice conveniently; in harvest, and other busy times, demands the pot to be boiled only on a Sunday; has twice as much strength in it as any other thing of the same weight; and in short, has in it every quality that tends to make a labourer's family able to work . . .

William Cobbett

William Cobbett was preaching to the converted when he wrote his long chapter on the cottager's pig in 1821; the pig had already been part of rural economy for nearly two hundred years and only ceased to be when it became illegal to keep a pig too near the house.

Pigs should be killed from November to March, during the coldest part of the year. They should be rested and fasted for twenty-four hours beforehand, but allowed plenty of water.

The ideal pig is long in back and in ham, small in shoulder and not overfat—but not overlean, either, as the modern breeds are rapidly in danger of becoming; in addition the over-fast maturing that is part of today's methods of pork production gives dry, flabby and flavourless meat—certainly nothing that Cobbett would have recognised.

Dec 7. Nancy's Pigg was killed this Morning and a nice, fine, fat White Pigg it is. It is to be weighed to Morrow Morning. We are to make some Somersett black Puddings to Morrow.

The Rev James Woodforde, c1790

Recipes

Black Pudding

This is the baking-tin variety, which was often made as an alternative to the laborious task of filling the skins.

1 quart pig's blood	¼ lb chopped onion
1 quart milk	¼ lb oatmeal
¾ lb stale breadcrumbs	2 heaped tblsps salt
1 lb back fat	1 heaped teaspoon black pepper
½ lb barley	½ teasp allspice
	3 teasps dried sage

Strain the blood into a bowl and stir to prevent clotting. Cook the barley and strain. Pour the milk over the breadcrumbs. Chop the fat finely. Mix all the ingredients and seasoning and bake in a moderate oven in a greased roasting tin.

Cumberland Sausage

This recipe was given to me by someone who had worked in the butchery department of the Cumbrian Co-op for many years. It is the simplest and, I think, the best of all British bangers and contains *no cereal at all*.

> 1 stone finely chopped pork, fat and lean mixed with the bias towards the fat
> 2 oz white pepper
> 4 oz salt

Mix well and use to stuff skins about 1½'' in diameter—do not twist into links. One theory for the lack of links in Cumberland sausage is that when made it would be hung up on a hook in the kitchen, and members of the household would cut off as much as each person's appetite required.

Faggots

The liver, kidneys and smelt boiled together, bread soaked in the liquor, plus sage and onion. Mixed together, put in a roasting tin, cover with the veil from the chitterlings, and roast.

Every last scrap of pork was chopped up small and cooked in a low oven with mace, cloves, pepper and salt and a little water; this eventually set to a jelly. I make the French version of this, *rillettes*, by chopping scraps of pork and cooking them with garlic and herbs and a little wine or water in a very low oven overnight. The difference is that the *rillettes* are thoroughly drained of any liquid, then chopped again and potted with a lid of lard, to keep for several months.

Jean's Brawn

One of those accidental recipes which often turn out so well. Jean had no sage, so flung in a handful of sage-and-onion

124

stuffing mix instead—it gave the brawn a particularly good, slightly crumbly texture, much more attractive than the solid slabs so offputting to brawn-haters.

Leave a split pig's head in brine for 24 hours, then in vinegar for 12 hours (or overnight). Rinse it, then put in a large pan with flavouring herbs and vegetables and a dessertspoon of peppercorns, cover with water and bring to the boil. Skim the pan, lower the heat and leave to simmer gently until the meat is falling from the bones—from 2–3 hours. Remove the meat from the pan and chop it roughly, and pack it into pudding basins rinsed with cold water. Strain the cooking stock, add a generous handful of sage-and-onion stuffing mix (optional but good), and simmer fast until the liquid is reduced by about half. Taste for seasoning, cool a little, then pour over the meat in the basins and leave to set. Turn out to serve, with pickles and salad.

Curing Hams

Dry Cure

You will need a stone slab, or a large solid wooden board, or, best of all, an old stone sink, for the salt-bed; this should be placed in a cool, dry place, preferably dark as well. For every 100 lbs of pork you will need 10 lbs of salt and 3 oz saltpetre, plus extra salt for the salt-bed. Brown sugar can be added (2 lbs to every 10 lbs salt) to counteract the hardening action of the saltpetre and to improve the flavour. Divide the mixed salt, saltpetre and sugar into three. Make a strong brine from another 13 lbs salt to 5 gallons water, boiled together and cooled completely, then soak the meat to be cured in this for an hour to cleanse it. Wipe the meat with a boiled cloth, and rub ⅓ of the dry cure mixture into the rinds of the meat until it sweats (traditionally, the pig's ears

125

were used for this operation); spread an inch of salt on the salt-bed and arrange the meat on this, rind down, keeping the various joints separate. Sprinkle the second ⅓ of the mixture over the flesh side of the meat, rubbing well in round any bones. Fill in gaps between the joints with extra plain salt to exclude the air, and cover with a layer of salt. Leave for a week, then remove the meat and throw away any discoloured salt. Sprinkle again with the remaining ⅓ of the cure mixture which should have been stored in a dry place and re-cover with plain salt. The time the joints remain in the salt depends on the thickness of the joint: 3–4 days per inch thickness of meat is a mild cure and suitable for most tastes.

To store, remove the cured joints, wash them well under cold running water, wipe with boiled cloths and hang the meat up to dry. You can then either wrap the dry joints in old clean (boiled again) pillowcases, or in muslin, which you can then paint with lime-wash. Store in a cool, dark room. They will keep for at least six months.

Suffolk Cure

Dry salt the hams for a week by the above method, then immerse them in a sweet pickle made from 2 lbs black treacle, 2 lbs dark brown sugar, 2 pints stout, heated together and allowed to cool. Turn the ham in this, daily, for 6 weeks before smoking it.

Smoking Hams

This domestic method comes from *The Smallholder's Year Book* for 1923. You need 1 cider cask or large barrel, an old bucket, and some bricks. Screw a strong hook into the inside of the top of the barrel and suspend the ham from it. Dig a hole in the ground, make holes in the bucket and place it in the hole; put a layer of red hot cinders in the bottom, then cover with plenty of sawdust (oak for preference, *not* fir or deal). Damp it a little to prevent flaming. When smoking well, stand the barrel over the bucket for 48 hours, adding more sawdust if and when necessary. If it is not possible to dig a hole, surround the bucket with bricks and stand the barrel on these.

Baking Hams

The old method of baking a ham was to make a 'huff' paste from coarse meal and water, enclose the ham in this and bake it slowly in a bread oven. The crust was broken away from the ham (and fed to the pigs), the skin removed and the fat scored into 1″ squares. A clove was stuck into each alternate square, the whole was dredged with brown sugar and glazed in a hot oven.

The modern method is to soak the ham for 24 hours, changing the water twice. Make a paste with 2½ lbs flour and water to bind, roll this out and enclose the ham completely, damping and pinching all edges until the parcel is thoroughly sealed. Put the ham on a large baking sheet and into a hot (425°F) oven for 20 minutes, then lower the heat to 350°F and continue to bake for 30 minutes to the pound. The ham can then be finished as above.

Finish your home-cured and home-baked ham with a ham frill, very simple to make, but needing a band to hold it in place. Make this from a 5″ long, 2″ wide strip of white cotton or linen; neaten the two short edges and stitch channels along the long sides. Run drawstrings through these channels. Make the frill itself from a 6″ square of stiff white paper; fold it in half and cut in ¼″ wide strips from the fold to within 1″ of the opposite edge. Open out and fold the other way out to form a frill. Wrap this round the shank bone and tie tightly in place with the cotton grip band.

🌿 *Goats* 🌿

Nothing is so hardy; nothing is so little nice as to its food. They will eat mouldy bread or biscuit; fusty hay, and almost rotten straw, furze-bushes, heath-thistles; and, indeed, what will they not eat when they will make a hearty meal on *paper*, brown or white, printed on or not printed on, and give milk all the while.

William Cobbett

Goats will also stop at nothing, and need firm tethering or fencing.

Goats' milk was thought better for babies than cows' milk as it is less liable to bacterial infection.

🌿 *Sheep* 🌿

Time was when ewe-milking created a great stir in the farm-house in the making of ewe-milk cheeses; and so much anxiety did housewives evince for this process, that the ewes were milked until they were perfectly lean, to supply a sufficiency of this sort of milk—It was misplaced economy to reduce the condition of the entire ewe-flock for the poor boast of making a few strong-tasted cheeses.

Henry Stephens, 1855

Ewes were sometimes milked after the lambs had been weaned. True Rocquefort cheese is made from ewes' milk, not a cheese to have pleased Henry Stephens.

Sheep make excellent lawn mowers as long as they are kept away from other plants—sheep-bitten turf is smooth and level, and the droppings form a rich manure.

In mountainous areas of Wales, Scotland and the Lake District, mutton hams and sausages replaced the pork of lowland areas. The hams can be cured in the same way as pork hams, but for a shorter time.

As with the pig, all that was left unused of the sheep's carcase was the bleat. Many containers were made from the horns, from drinking vessels to medicine and ink bottles; the horn was also used in lanterns, and for buttons, spoons and forks, and many other household items. In Wales, harp-strings were made from sheep-gut. Tallow was used for lighting, for greasing leather harness, boots, and saddles. Wool, however, was the all-important product.

It is the office of a Husbandman at the sheering of his sheep, to bestow upon the House-wife such a competent proportion of wooll, as shall be convenient for the clothing of his family.

Gervase Markham, 1653

Lanolin from the fleeces formed the basis of many country ointments, and was collected by first washing the fleece in cold water, then boiling it until the grease floated to the top of the water. The tub was withdrawn from the heat and as the water cooled, the lanolin formed a thick white mass on the surface, which was skimmed off and kept. Farm labourers liming fields protected their faces, necks and hands from the effects of the lime by liberal applications of lanolin.

Sheep-shearing time was one of the annual festivals—a harvest of wool.

> Wife, make us a dinner, spare fleshe neither corn
> Make wafers and cakes, for our sheeps must be shorne.

Wild mint was added to the water in which the shearers washed their hands, to 'cut' the grease and eliminate the smell.

The other great event in the sheep calendar is lambing. A ewe has its first lamb when it has 2 permanent incisor teeth on the lower jaw (the top jaw is a toothless pad), its second lamb when it has 4 permanent teeth, and its third when it has 6. Eight incisors equal a 'full-mouthed' ewe—still capable of producing more lambs, but the teeth will begin to deteriorate. Arable farmers who fed their sheep on turnips would sell their thrice lambed full-mouthed ewes to pasture farmers as 'sound in tooth and udder'.

Ivy brought in to decorate the house at Christmas was fed to ewes to encourage the birth of twin lambs; ivy is in any case much liked by sheep—a sick sheep will seek it out and eat it as a dog will eat grass. Hazel catkins were brought into the house at lambing time as a good luck charm.

A good shepherd was one of the most important members of a farming community; he was considered a craftsman and was paid and treated as such. His skills were particularly vital at lambing time, when he would sleep out with the flock. Shepherds were traditionally buried in their smocks, with a handful of wool, as a passport to Heaven by reason of their trade.

A shepherd's smock (or 'slop', or 'round-frock') was made from about eight to nine yards of 'drabbet'—twilled linen drab, smocked across the chest and shoulders for both elasticity and warmth. It was pulled on over the head, as the lack of openings made it especially warm and windproof. Long pockets hung down inside to hold bottles of sheep medicine, or bottles of milk for orphaned lambs.

❧ *Hedging* ❧

The Hawthorn Hedge, and intermingled Crab; the brown Oak, and the elegant leaved Ash, all join to diversify the Scene in our most common Fences; and a Prospect from the most conspicuous Part of the intended Ground, over a cultivated Country disposed in Arable and Pasture Land, must also be agreeable. The good Growth of the Trees will also shew the general right Quality of the Soil.

John Hill, 1757

Hedges were valued not only for their ability to keep stock in, but also for the shelter they offered to the stock in bad weather, for their contribution to the beauty of the landscape, and not least for the wood they provided for various farm and household uses.

A very early method of hedge-planting was to plait into a skein of woollen cloth the seeds of whatever hedgerow trees and shrubs were required—thorn, holly, ash, oak, sycamore, etc. A ditch was dug, with a trench running along the top and the plait was buried in the trench. As the seedling trees appeared, they were severely pruned to encourage branching. The purpose of the wool was to act as a good fertiliser for the growing trees—a practice common amongst early gardeners. If this method was widely practised, it would cancel out the present theory of hedgerow dating, which calculates one species for each hundred years of growth.

Hedge laying is a reviving craft, fortunately, as a well-laid hedge is not only a thing of beauty, but an impenetrable defence, and a long-term investment. All dead wood should be cut out, and any brambles removed. The young, pliable wood is then cut three-quarters of the way through, about an inch above ground level, and either pegged down flat, or woven at an angle of about 40° between stakes and tied in place with a 'rope' of brushwood.

Brambles should be cleared from hedges in fields where sheep graze, as they will catch in the fleeces.

Cattle were thought to thrive in hawthorn-hedged fields.

Yew, as particularly poisonous to cattle, is weeded out of hedges wherever it occurs. It is traditionally the wood of the famous English long-bow.

Hedgers say it is unlucky to cut holly, so any required for whip-handles and walking sticks must be pulled out, rather than cut. It is a very solid wood and can make a dangerous weapon.

Birch, as a pliable wood, was used for brooms and baskets. A bundle of birch twigs, peeled and washed, was used to whip egg whites and cream, or any mixture which needed air to be incorporated. I have such a bunch and it is surprisingly effective for certain tasks, such as folding sugar into meringue mixtures, or flavouring into syllabubs.

Willow, of course, provides material for baskets and cricket bats, and for the slats of water-wheels. Willow-bark soaked in vinegar is one of the many cures for warts.

To Make a Walking Stick

Choose a straight sapling or branch, about 3/4'' in diameter, of holly (but see the preceding note), ash, or thorn. If you can find a stick which has tendrils of clematis or honeysuckle twined round it, it will have an interesting spiral effect. Cut it to the length you require, trimming it further once you have got it home, so that it is a comfortable fit. You can strip the bark, but it looks better left on. For a curved handle, choose a pliable wood and bend and tie it firmly, then leave for about 6 months. Trim it to a neat curve,

133

then sandpaper to a smooth finish. Season your walking stick by leaving for about 2–3 months before waxing or varnishing it.

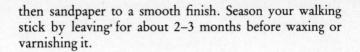 Weather

The weather is a vital ingredient in the fortunes of all who work in the country, and weather lore, handed down from generation to generation, has often proved more reliable than scientific weather forecasting.

Here is the pessimists' lore:

> The South wind brings wet weather
> The North wind wet and cold together
> The West wind always brings us rain
> The East wind blows it back again
> If the sun in red doth set
> The next day surely will be wet
> If the sun doth set in grey
> The next will be a rainy day.

A general Mist before the Sun rises, near the full Moon— Fair Weather.

Sudden Rains never last long: But when the Air grows thick by Degrees, and the Sun, Moon and Stars shine dimmer and dimmer, then it is likely to rain six Hours usually.

If the latter End of October and Beginning of November be for the most Part warm and rainy, then January and

February are likely to be frosty and cold, except after a very dry Summer.

The Shepherd of Banbury's Rules, 1827

If Janiveer calends be summerly gay
Twill be winterly weather till calends of May

Thomas Tusser, 1573

If small Birds prune themselves and duck and make a shew of washing, if Crows make a great Noise in the Evening, if Geese gaggle more than usual, these are all Signs of Rain, because these Animals love wet weather, and rejoice at the approach of it.

But the surest and most certain Sign is taken from Bees, which are more incommoded by Rain than almost any other Creatures, and therefore, as soon as the Air begins to grow heavy, and the Vapours to condense, they will not fly from their Hives, but either remain in them all Day, or else fly but to a small Distance.

from the notes to the 1740 edition of
The Shepherd of Banbury's Rules, 1827

General prognostics for high wind: when cattle appear frisky, and toss their heads and jump—When sheep leap and play, boxing each other—When pigs squeal, and carry straw in their mouths . . . When crows mount in the air and perform somersets, making at the time a garrulous noise—when swallows fly on one side of trees, because the flies take the leeward side for safety against the wind . . .

Henry Stephens, 1855

135

General indications of a storm: when the missel thrush sings loud and long, on which account this bird has received the name of the storm-cock.

If the last eighteen Days of February and ten Days of March be for the most part rainy, then the Spring and Summer Quarters are likely to be so too: and I never knew a great Drought but it entered in that Season.

In summer or Harvest, when the Wind has been South two or three Days, and it grows very hot, and you see Clouds rise with great white Tops like Towers, as if one were upon the top of another, and joined together with black on the nether Side, there will be Thunder and Rain suddenly.

The Shepherd of Banbury's Rules, 1827

☙ *Harvesting* ❧

The 'haysel' or hay harvest is taken from mid-June into July, depending on the part of the country.

The hay of the sown and of the natural grasses are certainly very different in appearance—the former is composed of the strong and stiff stems of the red clover and rye-grass, while the latter feels soft and woolly, and more odorous, on account of the sweet-scented vernal grass, anthoxanthum odoratum, always forming a component part. Natural grasses—are more nourishing to old stock than sown ones; and hence natural hay is best for cows and horses.

Henry Stephens, 1855

Aug 17. Begun shearing my Wheat this morning and gave the shearers according to the Norfolk custom as under, a good breakfast, at 11 o'clock plumb cakes with carraway seeds in them, and some Liquor, a good dinner with plumb Puddings and at 4 beer again. NB the above are called elevens and fours.

The Rev. James Woodforde

Gloves were also part of the bargain for medieval harvesters—essential equipment when thistles grew thick amongst the corn. When more efficient methods of eradicating the thistles were found, the custom remained in the form of glove-money.

At length in Rows stands up the well dry'd Corn
A grateful Scene, and ready for the Barn.
Our well-pleas'd Master views the Sight with Joy,
And we for carrying all our Force employ.

Confusion soon o'er all the Field Appears
And stunning Clamours fill the Workmens Ears;
The Bells, and clashing Whips, alternate sound,
And rattling Waggons thunder o'er all the Ground.
The Wheat got in, the Pease, and other Grain
Share the same Fate, and soon leave bare the Plain:
In noisy Triumph, the last Load moves on
And loud Huzza's proclaim the Harvest done.

Stephen Duck, 1705–56, 'The Thresher's Labour'

Refreshments

Deals struck between the farmer and the team of harvesters would include beer in prodigious quantities (seventeen pints per day per man, according to one record).

Harvest Beer

3 lbs malt	2 large handfuls hops
3 lbs granulated sugar	5 galls water
3 lbs golden syrup	
1½ oz yeast	42 clean pint bottles

Boil as much water as you can in a large pan, with the hops tied in a bag; add the syrup and simmer for 45 minutes. Warm the malt and pour it into the fermenting tub, together with the sugar and the hot liquid (remove hops); stir to dissolve the sugar and add tepid water to make up the amount used in total to 5 gallons. Cool to lukewarm and add the yeast, cover and leave to ferment for about 5 days, removing the froth on top after the second day. Fermentation will have ceased when the froth subsides to a ring in the centre. Add a pinch of sugar to each beer bottle (omit this if you want a still beer), then bottle the beer. This is a strong brew.

Herb or Nettle Beer

1 large double handful young
    stinging nettles   or 4 handfuls of
1 large handful yarrow   nettle-tops
1 large handful sage
2 galls water
1½ lbs sugar
1 oz yeast

Boil the herbs in the water for 30 minutes, strain and add the sugar, stirring until it dissolves. Cool to lukewarm then add the yeast and leave for 24 hours. Strain, bottle and cork and leave for 3 days before drinking. This will not keep long.

For the 'gavellers'—the women and children who raked the corn into rows for carting—cold tea was taken on to the field, or apple lemonade: 2 large cooking apples, the rind of 1 lemon, 1 pint water, very little sugar.

Cut up the apples roughly without peeling or coring them, and put into a large jug with the lemon rind. Pour on the boiling water, cover and leave overnight. Strain and sweeten very slightly, although it is even more refreshing without any sugar.

Harvest Supper

> Then comes the harvest supper night
> Which rustics welcome with delight
> When merry game and tiresome tale
> And songs increasing with the ale
> Their mingled uproar, interpose
> To crown the harvest's happy close
> While rural mirth that there abides
> Laughs till she almost cracks her sides.
>
> John Clare, 'The Shepherd's Calendar'

The harvest supper, provided by the farmer, usually consisted of generous amounts of roast beef and vegetables, followed by plum pudding, plenty of cheese, and washed down with gallons of cider or beer. The following is a recipe for a very substantial harvest pudding:

Farmers' Choice Pudding

4 oz dried fruit	Pinch mixed spice
4 oz chopped apple	Juice & rind 1 lemon
4 oz suet	2 tblsps jam
2 oz brown sugar	Suet crust
8 oz stale breadcrumbs	8 oz flour
2 eggs	Pinch salt
Milk	Milk to mix
	4 oz suet

139

Make a suet crust with the ingredients listed, and line a large pudding basin with it; brush the inside with the jam. Fill with the remaining ingredients, well mixed. Cover with greased paper (note, no suet lid) and a cloth and steam briskly for 3½ hours, then turn the pudding out to serve. The donor of this recipe added this sauce to pour over it: mix 1½ oz ground rice with a little milk taken from ½ pint and bring the rest to the boil, mixing it with the ground rice and 1 oz brown sugar; simmer for 10 minutes, remove from the heat and stir in 2 tablespoons brandy.

☙ *Traditions* ❧

Harvesting

The last stalks in the middle of each field were made into the kern or corn dolly, as they were believed to contain the spirit of the corn. The dolly was tied with red threads against witches, and kept in the farm house to ensure continuity of growth, and prosperity.

The last sheaf from the harvest was kept to scatter over the newly ploughed fields in January as an offering for a good harvest.

Michaelmas (29 September) and Lady Day (25 March) are the traditional dates for changing farm tenancies— Michaelmas for arable farms (after the outgoing tenant's last crop has been harvested), and Lady Day for grass holdings (before the new season's grazing has begun).

The ricks were decorated by straws folded and tied into crosses, or crowns, or whatever shape the creator chose, as charms to stop witches flying overhead from landing on them.

Ploughing

Plough Monday was the first Monday after Twelfth Night, and there was often a race amongst the farmers to see who could get up and out into the fields first, as

> Plough deep, while sluggards sleep
> You shall have corn to sell and keep.

Plough Days, in January, were days when farmers from neighbouring farms lent their ploughing teams to any farmer who was unable to plough for himself. Nowadays they are days when ploughing matches are held.

A real ploughman's lunch was a hunk (or hunch) of bread and a piece of fat bacon or cheese if times were good, simply a raw onion if they were bad; there was no butter, and certainly no pineapple, a refinement I was given with my 'ploughman's lunch' at a pub in Kendal.

Hiring Fairs

These were the labour exchanges of the farming community, where a farm labourer tired of his place at one farm might find employment at another, and where farmers requiring farm hands might pick and choose among those seeking work. Thomas Hardy describes such a fair in *Far from the Madding Crowd*: 'carters and waggoners were distinguished by having a piece of whipcord twisted round their hats, thatchers wore a fragment of woven straw, shepherds held their sheep-crooks in their hands; and thus the situation required was known to the farmers at a glance.'

A 'Runaway Mop' was sometimes held two weeks after the Hiring Fair so that dissatisfied employers and employees might change their situations.

Let the wealthy and great
Roll in splendour and stare
I envy them not, I declare it.
I eat my own lamb
My own chicken and ham
I shear my own fleece and I wear it.
I have lawns, I have bowers
The lark is my morning alarmer.
So jolly boys now
Here's God Speed and Plough
Long life and success to the farmer.

A verse frequently applied to eighteenth and nineteenth century transfer ware jugs, mugs and bowls.

❧ Village Life ❧

Those of us lucky enough to live in an English country village will know that it is at once the most enjoyable and the most infuriating experience. If you have been brought up in a small rural community, you long for the freedom of the city and equally, if the tyranny of city streets has been your inheritance, you dream of the tranquillity of village life.

But village life has rarely been tranquil. Villages grew up to serve farms and estates, housing the craftsmen and labourers. The unceasing work involved in the farming year left little time for repose, and repose was in any case rare for the very poor, whose battle for existence was unrelenting. When life was not reduced to a battle with the elements, it was busy with whatever craft formed a livelihood for the householder. There were no short cuts then; everything required had to be made—farm implements, clothing, bedding, even kitchen utensils—on the estate. And when commodities

143

did become available, the work required to earn the money to buy them was as much as the work required to manufacture the items in the first place.

Only in the twentieth century, as large estates were broken up and sold off, as farming became increasingly mechanised, and the work reduced to tasks for 'two men and a dog' and sundry machines, did village life become tranquil. And that was because villages were in decay, emptying into the towns which could provide work. After the Second World War many books were written, and questions asked in Parliament, about the demise of the village and what could be done to revive them. The answer came naturally with increased prosperity—the second car, then the second home, which was often a country cottage bought cheaply in a village where the big house stood empty, the estate wild and un-kempt. More cottages were bought and refurbished, the big houses taken over as hotels or country clubs or health farms. Admittedly, the cottages stood empty for weeks at a time, waiting for their owners to leave town and pick up their country lives whenever they had time, and certainly prices began to rise, so that local people were unable to afford a house in their own birthplace, but at least a start was being made to re-inhabit and revive a once bustling community.

The villages we visited in our search for a house after our marriage in the mid '60s and rejected because they were dejected, mud-swamped and isolated, have grown—the old houses done up, new houses built, old barns converted. The effect is not always attractive, but it is alive, and village life is once again that irritating mixture of gossip and good neighbourhood, concern (or is it just plain nosiness?) and friendliness, with rarely a quiet evening as people drop in to discuss village matters and the next local event.

This chapter is a scrapbook of village life—odd pieces of information about the activities that went to make up the life of the English village in the last three hundred years. It really

144

needs a whole book to itself, but I have tried to collect pictures of the villages of yesterday, with a few references to the life of today.

Most villages grew up round one industry, that of farming. The village sheltered not only the farm workers, but also the craftsmen whose crafts and skills were required by the farms. Most villages of any size in nineteenth-century England could probably boast the following: blacksmith, coachbuilder and wheelwright, saddler and harness maker, carpenter, thatcher, stonemason, basket-maker, miller, and the subsidiary crafts such as shoe-making, potting, coopering, and hurdle-making. The women might make lace in one particular area, or gloves or buttons in another, to supplement the income of their husbands. In seaside areas knitting the traditional sweaters was the job of the women and sometimes of the older men, sail and net-making that of the younger men, again to supplement the income, this time from the sea. In cider-making areas the cooper would be of particular importance, producing the barrels. Straw-plaiting was practised, for the manufacture of hats— William Cobbett was very much in favour of this, devoting a whole chapter of his *Cottage Economy* to it: 'This straw affair makes an addition to the food and raiment of the labouring classes, and gives not a penny to be pocketed by rich ruffians.'

The ideal English village, from Goldsmith's *The Deserted Village*:

> The sheltered cot, the cultivated farm,
> The never-failing brook, the busy mill
> The decent church that topped the neighbouring hill,
> The hawthorn bush, with seats beneath the shade,
> For talking age and whisp'ring lovers made.

🍃 *Daily Life* 🍃

Pitiful it is to read the cottage woman's woe
Charged with a crew of children,
And with a landlord's rent
In the narrow room carding, combing, clouting
Washing, rubbing and winding, and peeling rushes.

Piers Plowman

Jack and Joan they think no ill,
But loving live, and merry still
Do their week-day's work and pray
Devoutly on the holy day;
Skip and trip it on the green
And help to choose the summer queen:
Lash out, at a country feast,
Their silver penny with the best.

Thomas Campion

Two pictures of village life, which, taken together, probably present quite an accurate one.

Washing late in the week indicated sluttishness by the un-written rules of the village—washing was done on a Monday, and bath night was Saturday. Bathing was done in relays, in a tub in front of the fire—whoever was last cannot have got very clean.

Soapwort (*saponaria officinalis*) was often used for washing when soap was unaffordable. It is very mild and especially good for woollens and for washing the hair. It is easy to

146

grow from seed, and is a pretty plant (native in the South-West and Wales). Cover a handful of the leaves with cold water and bring slowly to the boil. When the infusion feels sufficiently soapy, strain and use without diluting.

In hard water areas, the water was softened before washing by the use of an 'ash-cloth'. This was a coarse cotton or linen cloth tied across the top of the wash-tub, with a thick layer of wood ash spread on top. The water was poured through this and was thus softened as the ashes acted as a filter. A layer of mallow leaves was sometimes added to soften the water still further.

All water had to be carried from the well, or pump, and heated in a kettle over the fire. The more well-off households might have a copper boiler built in with a fire-mouth and a flue—these can still be seen (and used) in the outhouses or cellars of houses or cottages built in the last century. More usual were the large tubs and 'dollies' or 'possers' to pound and beat the dirt out of the clothes. The dolly is an implement that looks like a long-handled milking stool; the posser, also long-handled, has a copper bell at the end.

Life in farming communities was hard, particularly in the 1890s, when both work and money were so hard to come by that women were back in the fields within three weeks of the birth of their babies. The village midwife would be called in to help with the confinement, rather than the doctor, who was too expensive to be afforded by the poor (who in any case regarded his cures with some suspicion and preferred to rely on their own mixture of herbs, common sense and superstition).

Gruel, with a knob of butter and a pinch of ginger, was given to the mother immediately after her confinement, as a restorative. In Cumberland, rum butter was the post-natal tonic.

Breast feeding was believed to be a form of birth control; no conception could take place as long as there was a child at the breast. However, when it was necessary to wean a child, the mother's breasts were painted with an infusion of some bitter herb such as rue, or wormwood, to speed the process.

A pig-killing was a social event in the village which took place during the winter. Anyone who killed their pig 'in isolation' was looked on askance, as the aim was to kill the pigs at about three-week intervals to ensure a supply of fresh meat through the winter.

In some villages it was the custom to sit up all night with the carcase of the pig 'to see that the wolves didn't get it'; it was a good excuse for a party.

'Pig-cheer' was the name given to small presents of meat and offal to friends and neighbours, or to anyone who was sick or in need. Not infrequently a large proportion of the pig was 'owed' to various shopkeepers in payment of debts run up while the pig was being fattened.

Christening Chine
A particular cut (down each side of the backbone) which was often kept for christenings or other celebrations. It was

traditional for Mothering Sunday in Gloucestershire, and Christmas in Northamptonshire:

> And huswifes sage stuff'd seasoned chine
> Long hung in chimney nook to drye
> And boiling eldern berry wine
> To drink the christmass eves good bye
>> John Clare, 'The Shepherd's Calendar'

A Lincolnshire recipe for 'sage stuff'd chine' was to score the sides of a cured chine deeply and fill the scorings with a mixture of finely chopped parsley, marjoram, thyme, sage, young raspberry and blackcurrant leaves, leek tops and lettuce (all depending on the season). The whole was wrapped in a huff paste (see page 127) and baked at 325°F for about 25 minutes a pound.

Exchange and barter is still carried on within village boundaries; you swop your lettuce seedlings for strawberry plants, someone else lends a honey-extractor in return for the loan of a hedge-cutter. In the old scheme of things this method was called contra-accounting, with a proper 'Settling Day' once a year. There was often a scale of charges—coal or fuel would equal a joint of meat, dairy produce, groceries, and even, in some areas, a good funeral could be paid for in bags of horse feed.

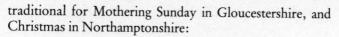

✌ *Fuel* ✌

Peat was the natural fuel in many areas, and was dug in summer and left in the open to dry, stacked on edge and turned frequently. In these areas, bread was often baked on an open hearth under a metal cover, the smouldering peat blocks piled round and over it to form a simple oven. Dark, heavy peat was slow to dry and burn, but gave out a better heat than the lighter peats which burnt more quickly. Peat stacks were usually thatched with reeds of bracken against the winter weather. Modern peat—a large industry in parts of Somerset—is used mainly for gardening, although a small proportion is made into blocks for fuel.

Cooking on peat—a good fire is built up with dry peat, and then damped down with wet peat. Keep dry peats round the fire to provide more heat when required. Again, as with bread, the flavour a peat fire gives to food is unforgettable; try using peat blocks instead of charcoal when cooking out of doors. For suppliers, the back pages of magazines such as *The Countryman*, or *Country Life* have useful addresses.

Charcoal-burning was a craft practised in old iron-smelting areas, and in hop-growing areas too, where the oast-houses were fuelled by charcoal. A shallow pit was dug in which lengths of wood were stacked in a pyramid. This stack was covered with a thick layer of soil and leaf mould, and a hole left in the centre. The fire was lit in the middle and kept under control so that flames would not break through the earth covering. The burning would continue for two to three days, then the fire was doused with water. When the mound was cool enough, the charcoal was raked out and stacked. The amount of charcoal thus obtained would be a quarter of the amount of wood burnt.

The standard of living varied from one part of the country to another. In the North, where coal was the cheapest fuel and this could be used to keep a stove 'in' all day, and where oats were grown which could be made into a sustaining porridge which even the poorest could afford, the quality of life was often better than that of the South, where all heating and cooking depended on a sometimes erratic supply of dry wood.

❧ Daily Fare ☙

The Three B diet, of Bread, Bacon and Beer, was the diet common to most cottagers, as George Ewart Evans points out in *Ask the Fellows Who Cut the Hay*, and all were produced at home. The corn was grown on the cottager's allotment until it was superseded by the potato in the eighteenth and nineteenth centuries, when the flour would be bought from the miller. Some of the more substantial cottages had their own bread oven, but there was usually a communal one in the village, for which each cottager supplied his own fuel.

This is the account of one labourer's diet, given to H. Rider Haggard in 1906: 'He stated that for months at a time he existed upon nothing but a diet of bread and onions, washed down, when he was lucky, with a little small-beer. These onions he ate until they took the skin off the roof of his mouth, blistering it to whiteness, after which he was obliged to soak them in salt to draw the "virtue" out of them. They had no tea, but his wife imitated the appearance of that beverage by soaking a burnt crust of bread in boiling water.—he became so feeble that the reek of the muck which it was his duty to turn made him sick and faint.'

Rural England

A family of ten used roughly five stones of flour, in two bakings a week. The oven would be heated by whatever the local landscape offered in the way of fuel—furze, heather, bracken, or twigs tied into faggots. Once the fire was lit, the oven took about an hour to reach the required heat—tested by throwing a sprinkling of flour into the oven: if it disappeared in a shower of sparks, the oven was ready. The ash was scraped out with the aid of a 'peel'—a flat wooden spade with a long handle that was also for sliding the loaves in and out of the oven. The cinders and ash which remained despite the action of the peel gave the bread a special flavour, which anyone who has tasted bread made in this way will agree makes even the best home-made bread insipid by comparison. Now that wood-burning has grown in popularity as an alternative to increasingly expensive gas and electricity, it is possible that this old method of bread-making might be revived by the small independent bakers.

Hefty food kept out the weather and boiled puddings which made the most of few ingredients and filled the stomach were common. The famous Bedfordshire clanger was one such—a long dumpling with bacon and vegetables at one end and jam or fruit at the other, tied in a cloth and well boiled. Such 'ribstickers' occurred in other forms—as dumplings in stews, or suet crusts on top of the stew, with cabbage steamed on top of that. Often a plain leek or onion dumpling might be had when there was no meat at all.

Another deservedly popular trick for stretching meat was to make a double-crust pie. The pie would be put in the oven first of all with a suet crust, and baked slowly to cook the filling. Then the suet crust would be pushed down into the gravy and a shortcrust lid put on and the pie returned to finish cooking at a high enough temperature to bake the pastry a crisp brown. The suet would absorb the gravy and add to the meat content.

Salt pork was an alternative to bacon, and was made by keeping the fatter joints in brine until they were required. It is very easily digested and was often recommended to invalids. It is something we always have in the larder, as it is a useful supply of meat which does not have to be thawed out before use. Cubes of salt pork can be added to enrich game dishes and beef stews, and a piece of boiled pork with pease pudding, or carrots and cabbage, is a lovely warming winter dish.

Brine

You will need a suitable container for the brine, and a plastic brewing bucket with a lid is ideal. Sterilise it as you would wine bottles, with sodium metabisulphate. Dissolve 3 lbs salt (ordinary cooking salt, not table) in 1½ gallons of water, and add 1 lb brown sugar, some whole spices tied in a handkerchief and 2 oz saltpetre. Boil this hard for 15 minutes, then leave it to get cold. When cold, pour it through a muslin-lined sieve into the brine bucket. You can then immerse your joints of pork. My own favourite is boned belly pork, but shoulder is good, too. The meat should be kept under the surface and for this I use a plate weighed down with a very clean, smooth stone. The pork will keep perfectly for as long as you need it, although the longer it has been in the brine the more soaking it will need before cooking, changing the water once or twice as it soaks. A thick blanket of mould may form, but the meat beneath will be perfectly fresh. When removing a large piece from the brine, bring the remaining brine to the boil again with another 6 oz salt and allow to get completely cold before returning to the bucket.

Food for Free

Poaching—was it a craft? It was a way of life for the very poor, who risked their lives to feed their families by this means, and great skill was needed both to elude the game-keepers who ruthlessly patrolled the huge estates and to snare the game.

A seventeenth-century recipe for attracting pigeons was a mixture of gravel or sand, old mortar or lime, cummin seed and saltpetre—pigeons apparently like the smell of cummin; the other ingredients are not explained.

Cottager's Pigeon

Pluck your woodpigeons and put them in a casserole, with sliced onions and several large cubes of salt pork or bacon, a large bunch of herbs, a little hot water and some salt or pepper. Seal the lid on the casserole with a strip of flour-and-water paste and cook very slowly for four hours.

Sparrows were unpopular in farming communities at harvest-time, so village lads would organise a sparrow hunt, shining lights on the ivy-hung eaves of buildings where the birds were roosting, and catching them in nets when they flew out in alarm. They were cooked by wrapping them in bacon, after plucking, and roasting them on a spit.

Thrushes were caught and eaten in fruit-growing areas, by similar methods.

Rook Pie

A popular dish, as they have a gamy flavour and can be very meaty. I used to be able to buy them from a game stall in Newcastle's covered market—remove the backbone as this makes them very bitter.

Skin the rooks (do not pluck them), remove the heads and backbones, and draw them. Cut the birds in half and arrange them on thick pieces of braising steak in a pie dish. Fill in the gaps with quartered hard-boiled eggs, season well, add a little gravy or stock, cover with a rich shortcrust and bake in a hot oven for the first half-hour, then lower the temperature and leave to cook for 1¾ hours.

Country Rabbit

Skin, clean and joint the rabbit and roll the joints in seasoned flour. Fry them in lard to brown them, then put them in a pot with enough boiling water to come level with the meat, and lay a thick slice of bread on top, a little thyme, salt and pepper. Cook slowly until the meat parts from the bones (about 1½–2 hours depending on the age of the rabbit), then stir the bread into the sauce to thicken it.

Cumbrian Hare

Skin and joint a hare and put its fore and back legs into a pot (save the saddle for roasting and the head and ribs for soup). Season the meat, add two small onions, peeled and each stuck with a clove, and a jar of rowan jelly (see page 80 for

155

the jelly recipe). Seal the lid on with flour-and-water paste and cook very slowly for 4–6 hours, depending on the age and size of the hare.

Salted Salmon

Salmon was (and is) heavily poached, and it was a brave man who would risk having this salted salmon hanging in his house unless it was freely given or honourably caught. Take a medium-sized salmon—about 8–10 lbs. Cut off the head and open it down the backbone; remove the guts and scrape well, but don't wash it. Rub the fish well all over with a mixture of 1 lb coarse salt, 2 oz brown sugar (optional) and 1 oz saltpetre. Add crushed juniper berries and allspice if you want a spicier flavour. Leave the fish spread flat under a weighted board for 48 hours. Meanwhile, peel 3 straight ash-sticks and trim them to the same length as the fish, boil them for 20 minutes, then dry them in a low oven overnight. Use them to stretch the fish into a kite shape, sharpening the ends to make them easier to push through the skin of the salmon. Hang the fish up in a cool and draughty place—the drying time depends on the weather, but 2 weeks should do for an 8 lb salmon. It can be eaten raw, like smoked salmon, or hot, like smoked haddock.

Legitimate hunting dates:

12 August—grouse shooting begins.

1 September—partridge shooting begins, and ends 1 February.

1 October—pheasant shooting begins, and ends officially on 1 February, but the shooting of the hens stops earlier.

Cubbing starts in August.

Fox-hunting starts about 1 November and ends in April when point-to-pointing begins.

Partridge Rummy

A popular Cumbrian shooting lunch dish. Roast the partridges, allowing 1 per person if small, carve them and arrange them on a dish. While they are still warm, pour over 2 sherry glassfuls of rum. Leave overnight. Next morning remove the partridges, wrap in waxed paper and pack wholemeal baps filled with watercress.

A Gammon of Badger roasted

The Badger is one of the cleanest Creatures in its Food of any in the World; and one may suppose that the Flesh of this Creature is not unwholesome. It eats like the finest Pork, but much sweeter.

Lay the Gammon in a Brine of Salt, and Water that will bear an Egg, for a Week or ten Days, then boil it till it is tender, and after roast it, strewing it with Flour and rasped Bread sifted, in the manner of a Westphalian Ham. Serve it hot with a Garnish of Bacon fried in Cutlets, and some Lemon in Slices.

Richard Bradley, 1753

Badger was obviously a popular dish, as I have found several recipes for it; badger hams were smoked over birch wood, and badger grease was felt to be a sovereign cure for rheumatism.

Hedgehog is supposed to taste like chicken, although its eating habits are very different. The old gypsy method of cooking it was to wrap it in wet clay and bake it in the ashes of the fire. When done, the hard clay could be cracked open and peeled off, taking the prickles with it.

157

Squirrel—the body was roast on a spit, wrapped in bacon, and the tail made into a stew. I think things must have been very hard to make a squirrel tail stew palatable. When my mother came to try and cook one during the last war, she was driven back by the fleas.

Hedgerow Provisions

Hedgerow foods added variety to cottage food, and John Clare paints a vivid picture of

> — dames in faded cloak of red or grey
> Loiter along the morning's dripping way
> In wicker basket on their withered arms
> Searching the hedges of home close or farms

In the following case the berries are elderberries

> Here the industrious huswives wend their way
> Pulling the brittle branches carefull down
> And hawking loads of berrys to the town
> Wi unpretending skill yet half divine
> To press and make their eldernberry wine
> That bottl'd becomes a rousing charm
> To kindle winter's icy bosom warm.
>   'The Shepherd's Calendar'

Blackberries have always been gathered and made into jams, jellies, wines and 'robs', but I found almost no mention of the uses made of hips and haws, except in wartime recipes. This rather confirms my view that it was the discovery that rose-hips were rich in Vitamin C that boosted their

158

popularity, and our great-grandmothers did not appreciate this fact enough to make them fond of the dry, sour, tasteless fruit.

Country tobacco was made from dried hedgerow weeds and herbs, nettles, coltsfoot leaves, comfrey, woodruff, chestnut, beech and walnut leaves were hung to dry. The tough centre ribs of the leaves were removed and the leaves soaked in honey and sprinkled with rum or brandy; wrapped in a cloth they would be pressed between weights for about a week. The resulting block of tobacco would be stored carefully in an airtight container; as much as required could be shaved off and rubbed between the palms, then used for filling a pipe (usually of clay, to judge by the number of broken bowls and stems which come to light in old gardens and allotments).

Traveller's joy, the wild clematis, was called 'boys' bacca' in Sussex, because boys cut the small wood in pieces to smoke like cigars.

❧ *Education* ☙

None but imprison'd children now
Are seen where dames with angry brow
Threaten each younker to his seat
That thro' the school door eyes the street
Or from his horn book turns away
To mourn for liberty and play.

159

John Clare's schoolboys are newly returned to school after helping with the harvest—rural schooling was frequently interrupted so that the children could help with farming tasks. 'Brazzocking' holidays were given in Yorkshire, so that the children could weed out charlock from the young corn; Shropshire friends remember extra long summer holidays to help with potato picking—especially during the last war when labour was short. Harvesting, gleaning, hay-making, hop-picking and weeding were all reasons for being allowed (grudgingly) time off school.

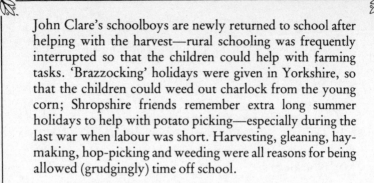

A good basic education could be had for a very small sum by the middle of the nineteenth century; it was considered important by those who wanted to better themselves, an unnecessary interruption to work to be done in the fields by those who were less ambitious. The poorer families needed their children's earnings and would set them to pick stones rather than learn tables.

Dame schools were run by one woman who taught for a small weekly sum—the schoolroom being a room in her own house. These have a long tradition—John Clare's schoolboys were attending one at the beginning of the nineteenth century and I and my sister went to two different ones in the middle of this century. I do not remember learning anything except how to play 'I sent a letter to my love', yet that cosy but strict régime must have taught me how to read and write.

3 barleycorns	make	1 inch
4 inches	,,	1 hand
12 inches	,,	1 foot
3 feet	,,	1 yard
6 feet	,,	1 fathom
5 yards and a half	,,	1 rod, pole or perch
40 poles	,,	1 furlong
8 furlongs	,,	1 mile
3 miles	,,	1 league
60 miles	,,	1 degree

This table may look a little odd, but every horse-mad child knows that 1 hand = 4 inches, and Parson Woodforde used the same table to measure the height of his wheat: 'July 9 Monday—Mem. A Stalk of Wheat (from a Field that was formerly a Furze-Cover) I measured this Morning, and it was in Length six feet seven inches and about a barley corn.' (Diary, 1792)

❧ *The Church* ☙

Village life centred as much round the church as it did around the work of the farms. The links between church and school were strong and most of the village festivals, when not part of the farming calendar, were religious.

The vicar's wife had a great deal of influence in the village if she chose to use it, and her qualifications had to be high in order to help feed, clothe and nurse the poor and sick of the parish. Whole books were published to help her do this, and recipes for feeding the poor copiously and cheaply occur in all Victorian cookery books:

The water in which meat has been boiled makes an excellent soup for the poor, by adding to vegetables, oatmeal or peas.

Mrs Rundell, 1818

From the same book comes this recipe for 'Portable Soup', or soup cubes, which could be kept in store by the thrifty housewife and used for the sick, poor and old: 'Boil one or two knuckles of veal, one or two shins of beef, and three pounds of beef, in as much water only as will cover them. Take the marrow out of the bones, put any sort of spice you like, and three large onions. When the meat is done to rags, strain it off, and put it into a *very* cold place. When cold, take off the cake of fat (which will make crusts for servants' pies), put the soup into a double-bottomed tin saucepan, and set it on a pretty quick fire—It must boil fast and uncovered, and be stirred constantly, for eight hours. Put it into a pan, and let it stand in a cold place a day; then pour it into a round soup china-dish, and set the dish into a stew-pan of boiling water on a stove, and let it boil, and be now and then stirred, till the soup is thick and ropy; then it is done enough. Pour it into the little round part at the bottom of cups or basins turned upside down, to form cakes; and when cold, turn them out on a flannel to dry. Keep them in tin canisters, when they are to be used melt them in boiling water; This is very convenient in the country, or at sea, where fresh meat is not always at hand; as by this means a basin of soup may be made in five minutes.'

162

Calves' foot jelly was considered a 'genteel' dish for the sick of the middle classes, while 'brewis' was thought quite adequate for the labouring classes and consisted simply of bread dipped in the fat on top of boiling salt beef or pork, the salting process making the fat digestible, but at the same time nutritious.

The village churchwardens were, and continue to be, drawn largely from the farming classes. Their job was the longer term care of the poor, raising funds to that aim; they had special dispensation to sell ale on Sundays and at Whitsun and Easter to raise money. They could coerce the wealthier tradesmen to donate gifts in kind—clothing, coal and food, and their job was helped by the fact that donations to the poor salved many a guilty conscience. John Clare had a pretty low opinion of them:

> Churchwardens Constables and Overseers
> Makes up the round of Commons and of Peers
> With learning just enough to sign a name
> And skill sufficient parish rates to frame
> And cunning deep enough the poor to cheat
> This learned body for debatings meet.
>
> 'The Parish'

Church Tea for 80:

5 gallons tea, 5 oz tea per gallon.
6 gallons coffee, half hot, half iced, 8 oz coffee per gallon.
3 gallons claret-cup—for each gallon, 4 bottles claret, 4 bottles soda water.
12 quarts water ices.

12 dishes sandwiches, all different.
8 plates rolled bread and butter, 4 brown, 4 white.
8 lbs cake, cut up into small thick pieces.
6 lbs sponge finger biscuits, freshly made at home.
Fruit salad always popular, ditto syllabub.

This must have been a very superior church.

Parkin

As sold in the tearoom of Quarry Bank Mill, Styal.

1 lb plain flour	1 lb black treacle
1 lb wholemeal flour	½ lb lard
1 lb medium oatmeal	1½ pints water
¾ lb brown sugar	4 teasps mixed spice
½ lb currants (optional)	3 teasps ground ginger
1 lb golden syrup	2 teasps bicarb. soda

Line 2 large roasting tins with greaseproof paper and heat the oven to 325°F. Put the water in a large pan with the syrup, treacle and lard and heat gently until the lard has melted. Mix all the other ingredients (except the soda) in a very large bowl and make a well in the centre. Add the bicarbonate of soda to the water/syrup/lard mixture and stir it until it froths, then pour it on to the well in the dry ingredients, mixing as you do so. Continue to stir hard until all the ingredients are incorporated, then pour into the roasting tins. Bake for about 1 hour, or until firm and springy. Cool in the tin. Each tin should cut into about 20 squares, which need not be large as this is a filling cake. It is at its best about a week after baking.

Tithe-audit dinners were lavish affairs held by the church to soothe the villagers and farmers who had had to give tithes to the church during the year. Every tenth animal and tenth fruit or vegetable, the milk of every tenth day, every tenth stook at harvest time, was supposed to be handed over to the church—in fact, money was often left to the clergy in the wills of farmers who had accumulated unpaid tithes.

Dec 4 Tuesday. This being my Tithe-Audit-Day—We had for Dinner a fine Loin of Beef rosted, a large Piece of Boiled Beef, boiled Leg of Mutton and Capers, Salt Fish, a Couple of Rebbits boiled and Onion Sauce and plenty of plumb and plain Puddings. Wine, Punch and very capital strong Beer to drink after. Three large Bowls of Punch, 4 Bottles of Rum, one Dozen of Lemons &c—it was the most agreeable Audit I ever had. None were asked to drink Tea, this time, as I thought improper so to do to introduce all kinds of People to my Niece and having no other Woman with her.

The Rev James Woodforde, 1792

Tithe maps are a fascinating source of information about a locality; they usually show and name individual fields, with descriptions of the crops growing in them at the time the map was drawn up. Each parish church has the local tithe map among its parish records.

The fifth week after Easter was Rogationtide, when the parish bounds were beaten. This antique custom involved a procession of bishop or priest, certain villagers, usually churchwardens, and the parish schoolchildren. All carried peeled willow wands topped with bunches of spring flowers, and the procession would walk the parish boundary, stopping at each familiar landmark at which the priest would say a blessing, or 'rogation'. George Herbert, in *The Country*

Parson, gave the following reasons why Rogationtide should continue to be observed:

1 A blessing of God for the fruits of the field.
2 Justice, in the preservation of bounds.
3 Charitie, in loving walking and neighbourly accompanying one another, with reconciling of differences at that time, if they be any.
4 Mercie, in relieving the poor by a liberal distribution of largess, which at that time is or ought to be used.

❧ *Village Fêtes* ❧

Village fêtes are one of my favourite forms of entertainment, whether I am involved or not. It is the only time I can be persuaded to buy lumpy knitted toys or lurid home-made sweets, and certainly the only time when I can be bullied into producing lumpy knitting or lurid sweets myself. Here are one or two ideas:

Jams, pickles and chutneys—if you are unsure of the quality of the contents, jolly the jar up with a decorative label and a frilly gingham top. The purchasers are liable to give them away untasted in any case, so with any luck your produce will not be eaten within the bounds of your village at all.

Home-made sweets—I give recipes for some opposite, but if time is short, buy dates, remove the stones, and stuff them with marzipan. Use pleated paper sweet cases as they make any confection look better, no matter how shapeless. Old date boxes lined with pretty wrapping paper make good packaging.

Offer to run a magazine stall—and get rid of all your old copies of out-of-date magazines. They are surprisingly popular, whatever the subject.

Or run a herb stall—grow some in pots, sell dried ones in cotton bags, make herb vinegars and hair rinses and put them in all the bottles you have ever kept as too pretty to throw away.

Sugar Mice

Or sugar apples, depending on your dexterity.

2 lbs granulated sugar	Cochineal
¾ pint water	White string or wool
3 oz glucose	Apple pips
Blanched almonds	

Put the sugar and water in a pan, heat to dissolve the sugar, add the glucose and boil to 240°F, or the soft ball stage (a little of the syrup dropped in a cup of water will form a soft ball). Take off the heat and cool until the mixture begins to thicken, then turn it out on to a cold surface—marble is best, if you have any, or a large sheet of glass—and when the mixture is cool enough to handle, work in a few drops of cochineal until you have a firm and opaque paste. Take lumps the size of a small egg and shape into pear-shapes, flattening the base. Push in a length of wool at one end for the tail, and apple pip eyes and almond ears at the other; if you have a pastry brush that is shedding its bristles, these make wonderful whiskers, but they should be removed before the mouse is eaten.

If you choose to make the apples, roll the egg-sized pieces into balls and flatten them slightly at top and bottom. Use real apple stalks, and paint cochineal streaks from the stalk

167

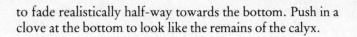

to fade realistically half-way towards the bottom. Push in a clove at the bottom to look like the remains of the calyx.

Cottage Candy

These melt if kept too long, but they are fun to do and are the 'sugar walking-sticks' once stocked by every village shop.

> 2 parts golden syrup to 1 part water
> Peppermint essence

Boil the syrup and water to the hard ball stage (a drop will form a hard ball when dropped into a cup of cold water), 280°F, take off the heat and cool until thick. Turn it out on to the marble glass slab (see preceding recipe) and when it is cool enough, divide the mixture into 2. Dust your hands with icing sugar and knead the ball of toffee, pulling it up into strands, kneading again and pulling repeatedly until it becomes opaque. Do the same with the other half, but knead in a few drops of the essence at the same time. Roll pieces of the two candies into long sausage shapes and twist them together, cut them into 10″ lengths and curve the top to form a walking stick. Once they are hard, stand them in a jar.

Fizzy Toffee

Very popular at our village bonfire.

> 6 oz granulated sugar
> 2 tblsps golden syrup
> 1 oz butter
> 1 teasp bicarbonate of soda

In a *large* pan, cook the sugar, syrup and butter together, once the sugar has dissolved, for 7 minutes, or until it has reached the hard ball stage. Take the pan off the heat and stir in the bicarbonate of soda—it will froth up in a spectacular manner, which is why you need a large pan. Pour into an oiled baking tin and break it into bits when cold. It doesn't keep, but rarely needs to.

Flower and produce shows need a higher standard of presentation—the vast vegetables, polished and perfect, the sculpted and scentless hybrid teas, clear wines and jellies, marbled jams and scones with burnished tops, the cakes shrouded in lingerie-coloured icing, the intricately knitted matinée jackets, all take weeks of careful preparation. The coward's way out is to push your children to the fore—enter the family guinea-pig in the pet show, or help them with a miniature garden for the 'industrial' section. If you have made a number of different jams, you can enter the baking class with one of those wonderful lattice tarts, with a different jam in each division. Bottled fruit can look good and win prizes, if you:

Use a light syrup—this alters the colour less than a heavy one; about 8 oz sugar to 1 pint water.
Choose evenly sized fruit.
Arrange halved fruit, like plums, with the halves facing out, against the glass. For extra chic, put a grape or cherry in the hollows left by the stones.
Polish the jars until they sparkle, and label neatly and clearly, with all the details.

ᛃ Country Crafts ᛒ

Country crafts are undergoing a welcome revival, not just as hobbies for long winter evenings, but as livelihoods for those brave enough to start out on such an undertaking. Modern life and its standardisations make us more appreciative of hand-made objects, particularly when they are of everyday use—my mother keeps me supplied with hand-made Sussex trugs for the garden as their lightness and durability puts them far ahead of any plastic imitation, and last week I had the pleasure of buying a new shopping basket made from Somerset willow—its sturdiness will make it outlast all my previous factory-made bags. It is possible to buy a specially made bowl for a wedding present in one village, a bag of stone-ground flour in another, and to have an old iron grate repaired by the blacksmith of a third, and it is easy to find a smock-maker, or a hand-framed Shetland sweater maker, or a thatcher, in any one of the villages throughout the country. The best way of discovering such people is to visit a local craft fair where, among less attractive items, you will find the best local craftsmen.

🍃 *Shops* 🍃

The village shop was often simply the front room of a cottage, selling bootlaces and writing paper and allotment produce along with gossip and advice. Happily, as long as the rural sub-post offices survive, so will the village shop, whose stock will not have changed a great deal, except that it now stocks a few frozen goods if there is space for a freezer, and more convenience foods generally. The higher cost of petrol and the dwindling country bus services have given the small country shop a new lease of life, and what it lacks in cheapness it will more than make up for in convenience.

Villagers had other retail outlets for their produce—the 'pannier markets' in small towns, to which anyone could take their allotment or dairy produce and set up a stall. A few of these markets exist still—we visit one nearly every Saturday where, in a covered market, old ladies sit and offer for sale cottage garden plants, bunches of herbs, a few duck eggs, a boiling fowl or two, and, in spring, 'tussie mussies' like the ones I describe on page 30. From such stalls you will still be able to buy apples which have slipped through the net of Common Market regulations, and eggs of such variable sizes that no amount of selecting could make them fit into sizes 2 to 4.

The mobile shops which still travel the more isolated villages began centuries ago in the form of pedlars, who sold cloth, pins and thread, pots and pans and universal panaceas. When such commodities became available, carriers' wagons brought out creature comforts from the towns—candles, lanterns, soap, scented stationery, coffee, even hats and shawls. In the Home Counties, the London evening papers were printed in time to catch the carriers' deliveries round the commuter villages.

❧ Inns and Taverns ❧

The other centre of commerce in a village was the inn, where the publican might sell insurance, and where deals were struck between dealers and drovers, farmers and graziers, and where travellers could buy information with their ale. The alehouse was a very different establishment, lower down the social scale—a meeting place for labourers:

171

Beware that you do not knock your head against the smoke-blackened beams of the low ceiling, and do not put your elbow carelessly on the deal table, stained with spilled ale left uncleaned from last night, together with little heaps of ashes, tapped out from pipes, and spots of grease from the tallow candles. The old-fashioned settles which gave so cosy an air in the olden time to the inn room, and which still linger in some of the houses, are not here—merely forms and cheap chairs. A great pot hangs over the fire, for the family cooking is done in the public apartment; but do not ask to join in the meal, for though the food may be more savoury than is dreamed of in your philosophy, the two-grained forks have not been cleaned these many a day.

Richard Jeffries, 1880

Taverns and alehouses offered a casual drink, maybe a meal, and sometimes a bed in an emergency, but it was very rough and ready. Inns were committed by law to putting up travellers at any time of the day or night, but could not serve the casual drinker. Today, inns can provide drinks and meals, and pubs can offer beds; the innkeeper is still required, by the same law, to give travellers a bed for the night.

Country Customs, Magic and Superstition

However sophisticated our world may have become, superstition and custom still play a part. Many people can be seen to hesitate before walking underneath a ladder, many listeners to the PM programme on Radio 4 admitted to saying 'White Rabbits' on the first of each month, when the point was discussed earlier this spring. I am frequently caught picking up pins from the floors of changing rooms in clothes' shops—I do attract some odd looks from those of my fellow customers too young to know the old rhyme, 'see a pin and pick it up, all day long you'll have good luck', but there are many who smile in agreement.

Superstition, magic and Christian belief together formed a complicated code by which country life was governed, at least for the uneducated. Crop failures, disease, poverty, were often as a result of 'ill-luck', rather than of man's own ineptitude; it is always a help to have a scapegoat, and if a

173

lazy dairy maid could blame 'the old witch' for her lumpy butter or soured cream, this would be likely to get her out of trouble with her mistress.

Old pagan customs and ceremonies were sagaciously adopted and subtly adapted by early Christian priests who saw them as the easiest way to persuade the rural population to take to them. This mixture of paganism and Christianity is especially obvious at the major festivals such as Christmas and Easter, in the greenery with which we decorate our houses, and the Easter eggs—fertility symbols given the significance of the stone at the mouth of Christ's tomb.

But despite the religious festivals and the Sunday church-going, witchcraft and magic continued to play a part in the countryman's life. It is easy to picture the scene Clare describes in the 'Shepherd's Calendar'—long winter evenings in front of the fire, whiled away with the telling of stories of witches and black riders, the studying of almanacs for signs and portents. The housewife 'knits or sews and talks the while'; 'And from her memory oft repeats, Witches dread powers and fairy feats'. Clare wrote his poem 'The Villager' in 1821, by which time steampower was used in factories and on farms. Nevertheless, the old man held out against any faith in such modern magic:

> His knowledge with old notions still combined
> — And thinks it blasphemy to be so wise.

> O'er steam's almight tales he wondering looks
> As witchcraft gleaned from old black leather books.

There must be many similar old people today who feel the same about computer technology—will computers and television make this the last generation of 'White Rabbits' mutterers and four-leaved clover searchers, or will superstition outlast these latest inventions, as it did that of steam and the combustion engine?

Most of the odd customs I have included in this chapter come from the novels, diaries and poetry of the period, although as many came by word-of-mouth. I found the museums of rural life were treasure houses of folk-magic, and would have liked to spend more time researching in this area, as so often one clue led on from another, and it was possible to trace a Christian custom back to its pagan roots. Among many others, I found the Museum of Rural Life at Glastonbury and the Folk Life Museum in Kendal particularly interesting.

⊌ *Winter* ⊌

Dec 24 This being Christmas Eve I had my Parlour Windows dressed as of usual with Hulver-boughs well-seeded with red-Berries, and likewise in Kitchen.

The Rev James Woodforde, 1788

The tradition of greenery in the house at Christmas remains from the pagan custom of welcoming the spirits of the woods into the warmth and shelter of the house.

Sterile holly, without berries, was considered unlucky, so it was combined with berried ivy; this combination was called the Holly Boy and Ivy Girl.

The kissing bunch has a far older pedigree than that of the Christmas tree, which was only brought to this country about a hundred and fifty years ago, by the Prince Consort. It is a great bunch of evergreens and mistletoe, decorated with red apples, oranges and candles. It is a northern tradition which could well be revived now that Christmas trees are becoming so expensive. To make one you will need a wire sphere—a spherical lampshade frame is probably the easiest way of obtaining one—and plenty of small evergreen branches; some red candles and holders, red apples and red ribbon, and a small bunch of mistletoe. Tie greenery on to the wire frame, hiding the wire completely. Clip seven candles to the frame at intervals (you can add another horizontal ring round the middle of the sphere, using a wire coat hanger and covering this with greenstuff as well; clip the candles to this if you prefer), and tie a red apple to hang beneath each candle. Hang the mistletoe underneath, and suspend the bunch from the ceiling—if you have a centre light fitting this is ideal, but make sure the candles do not reach too near the ceiling; they should be lit every evening from Christmas Eve to Twelfth Night. If your bunch is large enough, you can hang small presents from it as well.

Anyone kissed under the mistletoe should keep a berry, for luck in love.

All decorations must be out of the house by Twelfth Night (6 January), and out of the churches by Candlemas (2 February). Burning the spent evergreens on the house fire is unlucky—a good excuse for a mid-winter bonfire.

After I had gone to bed I saw from where I lay a bright blaze sprung up in the fields beyond the river and I knew at once they were keeping up the old custom of Burning the Bush on

176

New Year's Day in the morning—the whole valley can be seen early—alight with fires.

The Rev Francis Kilvert, 1877

The fires were lit to ensure a good harvest.

When it was still a cottage industry before the invention of the Spinning Jenny, spinning began again, after the Yuletide holiday, on 7 January, St Distaff's Day.

Winter is the season for those in the country reciprocating the kindnesses of hospitality, and participating in the amusements of society. The farmer delights to send the best produce of his poultry-yard as Christmas presents to his friends in town, and in return to be invited into town to partake of its amusements. But there is no want of hospitality nearer home. Country people maintain intercourse with each other; while the annual county ball in the market town, or an occasional charity one, to assist the wants of the labouring poor, affords a seasonable treat; and the winter is often wound up by a meeting given by the Hunt to those who had shared in the sport during the hunting season.

Henry Stephens, 1855

The Yule log was carried home in a procession; in Devon the 'log' was in fact a bundle of ash sticks bound with nine bands of ash-bark. Ash is widely chosen as the traditional Christmas wood and in Devon it was believed that Jesus' first bath took place in front of an ash-wood fire. When we trimmed some over-large branches from our ash tree this spring we were earnestly advised to keep the logs especially for the Christmas fire.

Wassail Bowl

(Wass hael—Your health—an Anglo-saxon toast)

2 pints good beer (page 138 for recipe)

Strip of orange peel, one of lemon, 6 cloves, 6 pepper-corns, a piece of root ginger, ½" cinnamon stick, ¼ nutmeg—all tied into a piece of muslin.

1 large spoonful honey

3 egg yolks

½ pint spirits of your choice—brandy, whisky, or rum

Put the beer in a saucepan with the spices and honey and bring it slowly to the boil, to bring out the flavour of the spices. Just before it boils, pour it carefully on to the beaten egg yolks in a large bowl, stirring continuously, then add the spirits. Keep the mixture as hot as possible without boiling, which will curdle it—a crock-pot will do this very well.

In Hampshire on Twelfth Night, twelve candlesticks, each representing a month of the year, were placed in line, with the candles lit. Each member of the household jumped over them and any flame which blew out represented bad luck for that month.

Childermas Day, 28 December, is a very unlucky day for the birth of a child.

🌿 *Spring* 🌿

20 March is the first day of spring because the Sun enters Aries on that day.

Collop Monday was the day before Shrove Tuesday; any remaining fresh meat was cut up and salted for Lent, and any fragments too small to salt were made up into 'collops' or rissoles.

> Pancakes on Shrove Tuesday
> Grey peas on Ash Wednesday
> You will have money all the year.

'Grey peas' are probably carlins, a traditional Lenten dish in Cumberland.

On Mothering Sunday, the fourth in Lent, girls in service were given leave to visit their mothers, taking a simnel cake as a gift. In Warwickshire, the traditional meal on this day was a chine of pork (see page 148), followed by fig pudding. This pudding was also eaten on Fig, or Palm, Sunday in the South.

Fig Pudding

12 oz fresh breadcrumbs	1 teasp cream of tartar
	2 oz flour
8 oz chopped figs	1 teasp nutmeg
4 oz suet	2 eggs
4 oz demerara sugar	½ teasp bicarb of soda
¼ pint milk	Pinch of salt

Mix all the dry ingredients, beat the eggs in the milk and add; beat all together thoroughly. Turn into a greased pudding basin and steam for 4 hours.

A piece of hawthorn brought into the house on Maundy Thursday will protect it from lightning through the year.

Good Friday Bread—there are many beliefs that bread made and baked on that day has magical properties; in Somerset it is thought that the bread will keep for seven years, and that a loaf hung in barns will keep the rats away. In Norfolk, Good Friday bread soaked in milk was a cure for dysentery.

Pace (or Peace) eggs can be seen for sale around Easter all over Cumberland—they are very hard-boiled and a beautiful shiny golden-brown from being boiled with onion skins (a little vinegar in the water also makes them shiny). They are rolled down a steep slope on Easter morning (and said to represent the rolling away of the stone from the mouth of Christ's tomb) by each member of the family; the owner of the first egg to arrive at the bottom intact will have luck and prosperity in the coming year. For the last fifteen years this ritual was somewhat confounded in our family by our labrador, who waited at the foot of the slope and ate the eggs as they came rolling down.

Easter eggs are hidden in the garden for children who believe (or are told) that they are put there by the Easter Hare. This is a complicated piece of mythology, but Bede thought that the festival of Easter came from the name of the Saxon spring goddess, Eostre, whose favourite animal was the hare. In American Indian mythology, the hare lays eggs like a bird (and it was a hare which was sent out from the ark to find the first piece of dry land). Weave all these strands together and you end up with that terrible creature, the Easter Bunny.

Sunrise services are still held in some areas on Easter morning, when the sun is supposed to dance with joy at the Resurrection.

Women could be lifted up (or 'heaved') by the men on Easter Monday; on the following day the roles were reversed and the women 'heaved' the men. It is unclear whether or not the second part of the custom came about with Women's Liberation.

14 April is the First Cuckoo Day; on first hearing the cuckoo, turn the money in your pocket.

> Cuckoo oats and woodcock hay
> Cause the farmer to run away

> If the Ash before the Oak doth sprout
> There has been or there will be, drought

Having always been brought up to believe that it is unlucky to bring flowering thorn, or may, into the house, I was surprised to hear of another superstition that maintains it is unlucky to cut down a thorn, but lucky to bring it into the house as it keeps ghosts at bay.

❧ Summer ❧

May Day was the first day of the Celtic summer, and May Queens, and Green Men (or Jacks-in-the-Green) shrouded in oak and hawthorn leaves were both fertility symbols which, like the maypole, were banned by the Puritans.

May Eve. Saturday. This evening being May Eve I ought to have put some birch and wittan [mountain ash] over the door to keep out the 'old witch'. But I was too lazy to go out and get it. Let us hope the old witch will not come in during the night. The young witches are welcome.

The Rev Francis Kilvert, c1870

In Devon, it is thought to be bad luck to wash blankets in May, which seems entirely understandable because of the temperamental temperatures, and is similar to the more familiar maxim, 'Ne'r cast a clout till May be out.'

A child born on Whit Sunday will die young unless it is named after one of the saints.

Never cut your nails on Whit Monday—nail-clippings were used by witches to prepare spells.

29 May is Royal Oak Day, a custom started when Charles II came to the throne in 1660, so it is relatively new as customs go. Oak branches were brought into the churches, men wore knots of the leaves in their hats, and horses, in their bridles. It is obviously the day to open a bottle of oak leaf wine (page 89).

Midsummer is the most magical of times, and a time when most love spells were cast; in Somerset, a snail put on a pewter dish on Midsummer Eve will trace out the initials of a true lover.

A rose picked on Midsummer Eve and kept until Christmas would stay as fresh as the day it was picked. If the picker wore the rose on her dress on Christmas Day, the one who removed it would be her husband.

Baal fires were lit on Midsummer Eve to worship and strengthen the power of the sun for harvest; the brand to light the fires would be passed from farm to farm in a westerly direction. In the north-west the cattle were driven through the smoke to make them immune from disease.

Before the Enclosure Acts of the eighteenth century, stock was put out to pasture on hay meadows at Lammastide, 1 August, until spring, when the grass was left to grow up to hay. This continues today, on common land, in some areas.

Lammas means 'loaf-mass'; the first loaf made from the first ripe corn of the year was offered at a service, to which the villagers brought a sheaf of the new corn as well as the loaf. This service now takes place on the first Sunday in August.

It is bad luck to pick poppies in cornfields, as they protect the crop from damage by thunderstorms, and are even called 'thunder-cups' in some areas. Although it is rare to see poppies in cornfields today, where they are found they do not seem very effective.

In Cheshire, the church bells should be allowed to ring three times over the stooked corn before it is carried off the field.

In Devon and Somerset, 'crying the neck' was the custom as the last stalks of corn were cut and plaited into the corn-dolly. The harvesters bent and touched the stubble, then stood upright, raising their hats above their heads, shouting 'The Neck' as they did so.

◈ *Autumn* ◈

This is a great *Nut* year. I saw them hanging very thick on the way-side during a great part of this day's ride; and they put me in mind of the old saying, 'A great Nut year, a great Bastard year.' That is to say, the succeeding year is a great year for bastards. I once asked a farmer who had often been overseer of the poor, whether he really thought that there was any ground for this old saying, or whether he thought it was mere banter? He said, that he was sure that there were good grounds for it, and he even cited instances in proof, and mentioned one particular year, when there were four times as many bastards as ever had been born in a year in the parish before; an effect which he ascribed solely to the crop of nuts the year before.

William Cobbett

Unmarried mothers who pulled cabbages blindfold on All Hallows Eve would be able to discern the looks of their future husband.

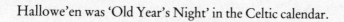

Hallowe'en was 'Old Year's Night' in the Celtic calendar.

All journeys should end before sunset on All Hallows; if this is not possible, then the traveller must carry a piece of bread on which salt has been sprinkled in the form of a cross.

A lighted candle would be left burning in stables all night.

In Lancashire, groups of people carrying lights would walk the hills around midnight. If the flames burnt steadily, then the bearers were safe for the year; if they went out, then they were blown out by witches—a very bad omen.

In Scotland, a bonfire was lit and when it had burned out, the ashes were spread into a circle and a group of stones, each representing a member of the household, was put in the centre. If any stones were discovered missing from the circle in the morning, then the person that stone represented would die within the year.

Apples, children and Hallowe'en crop up together in many superstitions. In Somerset, children went to bed with apples beneath their pillows, and bobbing for apples was carried on everywhere; a strip of apple peel thrown over the right shoulder would form the initial of a lover, on All Hallows.

185

🌿 Courtship and Marriage 🌿

> The even ash-leaf in my hand
> The first I meet shall be my man.
> The even ash-leaf in my glove
> The first I meet shall be my love.
> The even ash-leaf in my bosom
> The first I meet shall be my husband.

On St Valentine's Eve, pin a bay-leaf to each corner of your pillow, and one in the middle. If you dream of your sweetheart, you will be married within the year.

To find the name of a Valentine write the names of young men on small pieces of paper and wrap them in clay. Put the balls of clay in a bowl of water—the one that bobs to the surface first will be the Valentine.

A girl throwing hempseed over her shoulder on Midsummer Eve while standing in a field, will see the ghost of her future husband mowing the hemp:

> Hempseed I set, hempseed I sow
> The man that is my true love
> Come after me and mow.

Put an onion for each lover in a warm place near the fire; the one that sprouts first will be the bridegroom.

If twelve sage leaves can be picked on Christmas Eve at midnight without breaking the branch, then a girl will see her future husband.

A spell for 'young women'—mix wine, rum, gin, vinegar and water in a ground-glass bottle. Dip a sprig of rosemary in this on St Magdalen's Eve, fasten the sprig to your bosom and take three sips of the mixture. Prophetic dreams will follow . . .

In Wales and the Welsh borders, there was a curious custom called 'bundling'. The courting couple, both fully clothed and the girl wearing a 'courting-stocking', which enclosed both legs from the waist down, spent a night together, with a board down the middle of the bed.

A Sussex superstition has it that if a couple go to church to hear their own banns read, their children will be born deaf and dumb.

Marry in May		Marry in May
Rue for aye	or	You'll rue the day
Marry in Lent		And wed povertaie.
Live to repent		

Marry on:

Monday for wealth, Tuesday for health,
Wednesday best day of all.
Thursday for losses, Friday for crosses,
And Saturday no luck at all.

Myrtle is traditionally included in wedding bouquets (see page 19); if the sprig from the bouquet caught by the bridesmaid was planted and 'took', then her own wedding was near. This could explain the frequence of myrtle bushes in old cottage gardens.

White ribbons were tied to the bee-hives when there was a wedding in the family—bees should always be told of family weddings, births and deaths. For bees to swarm on a wedding day was a good sign.

It is lucky to be married on your birthday, if it falls on the same day of the week as the day of birth.

A flock of birds seen by the couple on their way to church foretells a flock of children.

Whoever falls asleep first on their wedding night, dies first.

In Orkney, marriages take place on a flowing tide.

> So many drops,
> So many knocks.

(A wet wedding day foretells a rough marriage.)

The rice now thrown at weddings used to be grains of wheat, the symbol of fruitfulness. In Nottinghamshire the wheat was thrown at the couple with the accompanying cry, 'Bread for life and pudding for ever.'

In Sussex, a 'bride-pie' was eaten at the wedding breakfast; it consisted of a whole chicken, stuffed with hard-boiled eggs, baked in a pastry crust, and symbolised fertility and prosperity.

🌿 *Birth* 🌿

In Derbyshire, the sex of the unborn child was foretold by blackening the bone from a shoulder of mutton in the fire, and hanging it up over the back door. The sex of the first person to cross the threshold the next morning determined the sex of the child.

To ensure a beautiful child, the pregnant mother should only look on beautiful things.

The earlier in the day a baby is born, the longer will be its life.

Midwives unlocked doors and loosened knots all round the house to ensure an easy birth.

A baby born on the stroke of midday will be simple.

Lucky charms:

In Devon—the baby should have its first bath in front of an
ash-wood fire (see page 177).
In Cumberland—the baby's head should be washed with
rum.
In Somerset—a bunch of primroses should be put into the
baby's cradle for luck. Dried or pressed ones were kept on
purpose.
In Shropshire—a baby's first taste of food should be of
butter and sugar to ensure a wealthy future. In
Cumberland this custom extends to rum butter, which is
served on pieces of toast to visitors after a birth.

It is unlucky for a baby to see itself in a looking-glass before
it is a year old.

🌿 *Death* 🌿

A loaf of bread containing quicksilver (mercury) floated on a
lake or river will float to the body of a drowned person.

Flowers with drooping heads portend death; as many of the
droopiest flowers appear in spring (snowdrops, hyacinths,
daffodils, etc), this may be linked with treacherous spring
weather (see May portents, page 182).

It is observed that if the chiefe person of the family that
inhabits in this farm doe fall sick, if his sicknesse bee to

death, there comes a paire of pidgeons to the house about a
fortnight or a weeke before the person's death . . .

Richard Gough

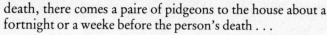

The unusual appearance of an owl near the house is another
portent of death.

Any bird down the chimney is a harbinger of death, particularly if it flies round the room.

A pewter dish of salt placed on or near the corpse symbolised
eternity, and fended off the advances of the Devil.

Yew, cypress and rosemary were once laid on graves, instead
of flowers. Rosemary was thought to preserve the bodies of
the dead, and was also the herb of remembrance.

The Nine Tailors are the nine tellers or tolls of the church
bell which tell of the passing of a man (six tellers for a
woman).

The corpse must be carried out of the front door feet first, or
his soul is in danger.

Sin-eating—a poor member of the parish would be paid to
sit near the corpse and eat bread, to absorb the sins of the
departed so that their soul could enter heaven.

Never whitewash houses in May, or death will follow.

In Hampshire, a crown was placed on the coffin of a virgin.

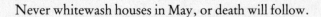 Miscellaneous Magic

Both iron and stone were powerful protectors against evil. Hag-stones—stones with holes through them—were valuable charms. We hunt for them on beaches as assiduously as we hunt for four-leaved clovers (and found one, one day, used as a fishing-charm, perhaps, as it had a piece of fishing-net attached). In Suffolk, hag-stones were hung over doors and windows to prevent witches from entering; sometimes a piece of iron was hung with it, as double protection.

A hag-stone exposed for three consecutive nights to the rays of a full moon was a charm to cure sickness.

Hag-stones hung over the bed warded off nightmares; carried in the pocket they protected the bearer against rheumatism.

A Sussex cure for ague, to be written on a triangular piece of paper and worn round the neck until it (the paper) dropped off:

> Ague, ague I thee defy
>   Three days shiver,
>   Three days shake,
> Make me well for Jesus' sake.

Any blade that causes a wound must be kept bright and free from rust until the wound has healed, or infection will set in.

I found many strange cures for whooping cough when I researched my last book, *Grandmothers' Lore*, but this is one I have come across since and is, I think, the oddest of all, although the logic can be appreciated—a few hairs from the dark cross on a donkey's back should be chopped finely and sprinkled on bread and butter, to be eaten by the sufferer.

Never apply ointment with the forefinger—called the 'poison finger'. The ring finger is the healing finger.

It is bad luck to see the first snail of the year crawling across a bare stone, but you can reverse the omen by picking the snail up by the horns and throwing it over your left shoulder.

Country people say that an adder can never die until sunset. If it be cut to pieces, the bits will retain their vitality till the sun goes down. They also say that on the adder's belly will be found the words—

> If I could hear as well as see
> No man in life could master me.
> *A Dictionary of Sussex Dialect*

The fat of the adder is the antidote to its bite.

The dried skin of an adder, hung over the door, is a preventive against fire.

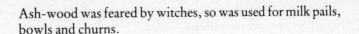

Ash-wood was feared by witches, so was used for milk pails, bowls and churns.

No butter should be made for winter use while the ash tree is dropping its leaves in autumn (a practical reason for this may be that the bitterness of the leaves may taint the milk).

A glass rolling-pin hung up over the hearth and filled with salt or sand delayed witches—they were forced to count the grains before going on their way.

Coloured glass, 'witch balls', hung as ornaments in cottage windows, deflected the 'evil eye'.

One of the explanations for the acorn-shaped knob on blind-cords, on curtain-rods and even on newel-posts, is that oak was a charm against lightning and fire.

Cutting hair at a new moon will make it grow thick.

Bread must never be burnt or thrown away (something that the manufacturers of electric toasters would do well to bear in mind).

Make all preserves at a full moon to obtain a full yield from the fruit.

In Somerset, boiling jam was stirred with rowan or hazel twigs to keep off the evil eye, and a cross was marked on each jar as further protection.

Pastry marked with hearts and crosses turns out particularly light.

In Sussex, mud is called 'January-butter' and it was lucky to bring it into the house in that month (I do not think my mother thought so), presumably because January is the month for ploughing, which is impossible in a hard frost.

> The magic wonders that deceived
> When fictions were as truths believed.
> > John Clare, 'The Shepherd's Calendar'.

❧ *Bibliography* ❧

Bradley, Richard: *The Country Housewife*, 1753 edition
Campion, Thomas (1567–1619): *Jack and Joan, They Think No Ill*
Carter, Charles: *The Receipt Book of Charles Carter*, 1732
Child, Mrs: *The American Frugal Housewife*, 1833
Clare, John: 'The Parish'
Clare, John: 'The Shepherd's Calendar'
Clark, J. H.: *The Cottager's Garden*, c1850
Cobbett, Anne: *The English Housekeeper*, 1851
Cobbett, William: *Rural Rides*
Cobbett, William: *Cottage Economy*
The Countryman Magazine, autumn 1947
Culpeper, Nicholas: *The Complete Herbal*, 1653 (1869 edition)
Digby, Sir Kenelm: *The Closet of Sir Kenelm Digby Opened*, 1669

Duck, Stephen (1705–56): *The Thresher's Labour*

Evans, George Ewart: *Ask the Fellows Who Cut the Hay*

Evans, George Ewart and David Thomson: *The Leaping Hare*, 1972

Evelyn, John: *Acetaria—A Discourse of Sallets*, 1699

The Gardener's Chronicle, 1849

Gerard, John: *The Herbal and Complete History of Plants*, 1633 edition

Goldsmith, Oliver (1728–74): *The Deserted Village*

Gough, Richard: *Antiquities and Memories of the Parish of Myddle*

Haggard, H. Rider: *Rural England*, 1906

Hardy, Thomas, the novels of

Herbert, George (1593–1636): *The Country Parson*

Hill, John: *Eden, or A Compleat Body of Gardening*, 1757

Jeffries, Richard: *Hodge and his Masters*, 1880

Kilvert, Francis: *The Diaries of the Rev Francis Kilvert*, 1870–9

Langland, William: *Piers Ploughman* (translated by J. F. Goodridge)

Markham, Gervase: *The English Housewife*, 1653

Markham, Gervase: *The Inrichment of the Weald of Kent*, 1675

Mauduit, Vicomte de: *They Can't Ration These*, 1940

Mawe, Thomas and John Abercrombie: *Every Man His Own Gardener*, 1829 edition

May, Robert: *The Art and Mystery of Cooking*, 1671

Nott, John: *The Receipt Book of John Nott*, 1723

Parish, W. D.: *A Dictionary of Sussex Dialect*, 1875

Ram, W.: *Ram's Little Dadoen*, 1606

Rundell, Mrs: *A New System of Domestic Cookery*, 1818 edition

Shakespeare, William, the poetry of

The Shepherd of Banbury's Rules, 1827 edition

The Smallholder's Year Book for 1923

Stephens, Henry: *The Book of the Farm*, 1855
Thompson, Flora: *Lark Rise to Candleford*
Travels Round Our Village
Tusser, Thomas: *Five Hundred Points of Good Husbandry*,
  1573 (edited by Dorothy Hartley, 1931)
Watts, Elizabeth: *The Orchard and Fruit Garden*, c1885
Woodforde, James: *The Diaries of the Rev James Woodforde*,
  1758–1802

ᔒ *Index* ᔒ

202

204